In Defense of
Political Reason

In Defense of Political Reason

Essays by Raymond Aron

Daniel J. Mahoney
Editor

Rowman & Littlefield Publishers, Inc.

ROWMAN & LITTLEFIELD PUBLISHERS, INC.

Published in the United States of America
by Rowman & Littlefield Publishers, Inc.
4720 Boston Way, Lanham, Maryland 20706

3 Henrietta Street
London, WC2E 8LU, England

British Cataloging in Publication Information Available

Library of Congress Cataloging-in-Publication Data

Aron, Raymond, 1905-
In defense of political reason : essays / by Raymond Aron : edited
by Daniel J. Mahoney.
p.   cm.
Includes bibliographical references and index.
1. Political science—Philosophy. 2. Liberty.
3. Totalitarianism. 4. History—Philosophy. 5. Progress.
I. Mahoney, Daniel J.
JC261.A7   1994   320'.01'1—dc20   93-48118   CIP

ISBN 0-8476-7877-6 (cloth : alk. paper)
ISBN 0-8476-7878-4 (pbk. : alk. paper)

Printed in the United States of America

∞™ The paper used in this publication meets the minimum requirements of
American National Standard for Information Sciences—Permanence of

Contents

Preface and Acknowledgments

To master the weighty corpus of Raymond Aron is surely a daunting task. In addition to the several dozen of his books on a wide range of topics that were published in Aron's lifetime, a half-dozen new and important works have been published since his death in 1983. And many new volumes of his journalism, classroom lectures, and unpublished and uncollected writings are bound to be published over the next decade or two. "Aronian" studies are undoubtedly a growth industry in France and the rest of the European continent (especially in Central and Eastern Europe where his works are rapidly appearing in translations) although the much respected Aron is more noted or discussed than read in North America today.

The remarkable Aronian renaissance in France, where Aron is the ascendant and relatively undisputed public philosopher of liberty, read and respected by the entire political and intellectual spectrum from the moderate left to the neo-Gaullist right, has barely caused a ripple in the faddish sea of the "social sciences" in the North American academy. This book, together with its companion volume, *The Liberal Political Science of Raymond Aron*, is intended to be a contribution to the correction of this relative neglect of one of the most penetrating political thinkers of the twentieth century.

Raymond Aron was the master of the short essay or *étude*. This fact is not always sufficiently appreciated. His magisterial works of scholarship such as *Peace and War* and *Clausewitz: Philosopher of War* are models of erudition and humane learning. But they are not immediately accessible to the preoccupied readers of our time, and the few who persist with the books do not always appreciate their manifold treasures and their unobtrusive sobriety and humanity. In a word, Raymond Aron wrote so much that many (sympathetic) readers do not know where and how to gain access to his wisdom. My suggestion is that Aron's shorter essays and studies provide the best introduction to the core of his work. In these pieces Aron confronts some of the most important political thinkers and issues of our time. We see Aron's ability to combine clarity and intellectual penetration, his remarkable powers of synthesis and evaluation, his scrupulous fairness toward thinkers with whom he differs. Above all, we see a practical illustration as well as theoretical defense of prudence or political reason. I have chosen important essays that are unavailable or relatively unaccessible or unknown in English—essays that illustrate Aron's efforts to defend political reason against various forms of irrationalism, determinism, reductionism, fanaticism, and doctrinarism. Without explicitly returning to the Aristotelian doctrine, Aron defended and embodies (in an albeit modernized form) classical prudence. Pierre Manent's elegant and authoritative account of Aron's life and thought which introduces this volume and my own brief introductory notes to the essays in question are intended to highlight this often unrecognized unifying focus of Aron's large and seemingly disparate corpus. I do not claim that Aron provided the definitive theoretical explanation of practical reason, but I do insist that his work is infused by that nearly forgotten and seemingly moribund perspective. The study of Aron's work and deeds can provide substantial material for a reinvigorated appreciation of the political perspective and of a social science that does justice to the moral dignity of the political vocation.

These essays have also been chosen because they do justice to the dizzying range of Aron's work. They help illustrate the architectonic character of Aron's reflection. They deal with the full range of his concerns, including political ethics, morality and international relations, the meaning of liberalism, the responsibility of intellectuals in a free society, and the contemporary crisis of democratic theory and practice. They also clarify Aron's intellectual affinities and indebtedness to, and important differences with, his two greatest teachers, Max Weber and Alexis de Tocqueville. Finally, these essays reveal Aron's "greatness" in fully comprehending and combating the totalitarian temptation. As these essays make clear, Aron remained a thoughtful partisan of the constitutional pluralistic regime and a penetrating and principled critic of all forms of totalitarianism, but he worried that liberal Europe was becoming less liberal and more democratic and decadent. Aron, however, refused to succumb to historical pessimism, the inverse of liberal or Marxist optimism, or to affirm the inevitable victory of Nietzsche's "last man" over the self-respecting liberal citizen and statesman. To the end, Aron remained a friend of human liberty, properly understood.

Aron can be considered the political philosopher of "1989"—of the victory of political moderation and liberty over ideocratic despotism. Yet he remains relevant after 1989. He is an intellectual antidote to any recurrence of the totalitarian temptation, and he teaches the democracies how they can be worthy of their unexpected and somewhat unearned victory.

This book is dedicated to my friend and teacher Pierre Manent, avatar and defender of political reason *par excellence*. His work is the natural and necessary supplement to Aron's: it shows us why political reason and the other "moral contents of life" exist in such attenuated forms in our "modern" and "democratic" world. I would also like to thank numerous friends who have stimulated my thinking and who have listened to my Aronian discourses over the years (I hope sometimes to have listened to them too): Jack Crutcher, Stephen Torraco, Terry Marshall, Philippe Bénéton, Peter Vedder, Rick Sorenson, Diana Schaub, and Dan and Lori Kelly. I would like to highlight the contribution of two friends in particular: Peter Augustine Lawler, whose advice, encouragement, and judgment are always invaluable, and David DesRosiers, precious partner-in-conversation and fellow-partisan of Tocqueville and Aron. Special thanks also to Marc LePain of Assumption College for his careful translation work and to my trusted friend Paul Seaton, also of Assumption, for his help with editing, proofing, and translating. Thanks and appreciation also to my friend and editor, Jon Sisk, my friendly and talented copy editor, Lynn Gemmell, and my wise, good, and generous parents.

Daniel J. Mahoney
January 1994

Acknowledgments

The essay *Raymond Aron: Political Educator* by Pierre Manent is reprinted by permisssion of Kluwer Academic Publishers from *European Liberty* (Martinus Nijhoff, 1983).

Max Weber and Power-Politics is reprinted from Otto Stammer, ed. *Max Weber and Sociology Today*, 1971 (with the permission of Blackwell Publishers).

The Liberal Definition of Liberty: Concerning F. A. Hayek's The Constitution of Liberty is published with permission from Editions Gallimard.

The essays *The Essence of Totalitarianism According to Hannah Arendt* and *On Tocqueville* are published with the permission of the journal *Commentaire*. The essay *For Progress* is published with the permission of *Commentaire* and the *St. John's Review.*

The essay *The Dawn of Universal History* is published with the permission of Librarie Plon.

The cover photograph of Raymond Aron is published with the permission of Agence TOP. The photo is by Edonard Boubat.

Raymond Aron—Political Educator

Pierre Manent

1983

Among the features that might characterize the XXth century—the one which begins in 1914—at least three are indisputable: [1] in the political field, wars and revolutions which seem to defy all reason by the discrepancy between the mediocrity of men and the scope of the events, by the duration of their destructive momentum which no longer seems to be controlled by any rational intent, sometimes even by the active presence of some malignant will which becomes an end in and of itself; [2] in the intellectual sphere, the separation of intellectual activity into varied disciplines which no longer have any necessary relation to each other, a specialization built upon the authority of that which we call science, however destructive of the organizing and integrating capacity of the human spirit; and [3] finally in the spiritual realm, the sway of a temptation, that of bidding adieu to reason. Martin Heidegger, the greatest philosopher of the century, who for some years lent his authority to the National Socialist movement and who, disdaining any *retractatio*, ceaselessly denounced reason as "the most relentless enemy of thought," bears witness to this temptation with emblematic clarity. When the last great representative of German philosophical thought makes an alliance with Acheron, when the communist movement in the name of the realization and the consummation of the Enlightenment restores the witch trials, how can one maintain one's reason? How can one protect the human city?

It is an instructive paradox that in the upheaval caused by his contact with a Germany toppling into darkness, a French Jew, faithful to the tradition of the Enlightenment, found the impetus and resources to confront the danger. The German experience protected Raymond Aron—although one had to be permeable to its lesson—from the liberal naïveté so widespread in France. By revealing the dependence of political events upon the adventures of the mind, it also saved him from the traditionalist and empiricist complacency to which an old

1

civic culture such as the Anglo-Saxon tends; in this particular case the German experience revived the Cartesian élan: the mind is not free as long as it is incapable of unraveling the long chain of motives that underlie events. With apparent effortlessness, Raymond Aron has maintained these three loyalties, tempered and enlightened by each other, to the German philosophic ambition, to the French intransigence and clarity and to the Anglo-Saxon civic spirit: this marks the breadth of his soul as well as the vivacity of his mind.

The Stages of a Life

Born in 1905 of an assimilated Jewish family from Lorraine, Raymond Aron received the education and followed the same academic curriculum as a number of "good students" who were to become famous after World War II: the Ecole Normale Supérieure (1924–1928), where he would meet Jean-Paul Sartre and Paul Nizan; his philosophy "agrégation" (1928); his stay in Germany (Cologne in 1930–1931; Berlin from 1931 to 1933). This visit led Aron to break with the dominant ideas of the academic circle of which he was a part in Paris. In this circle the two main personalities were Leon Brunschvicg and Alain [Emile-Auguste Chartier]. The former, a distinguished mind, retraced the history of Western philosophy and read therein the growing progress of rationality which he identified with science. He tended to consider that henceforth the task of philosophy was but to comment on the results and above all the procedures of science; he was hardly interested in politics. The second personality, an entrancing teacher, cruelly marked by his experience in World War I, developed anti-authoritarian political considerations, inviting citizens to always beware of the powers-that-be, to whom they owed obedience but never respect. Brunschvicg's political insensitivity and Alain's summary and literary politics did not help Aron to understand what was happening before his eyes on the other side of the Rhine. Other efforts were required to understand history and politics; other methods, another kind of knowledge than that with which university philosophers and partisan essayists contented themselves. To be sure, French sociology—the disciples of Emile Durkheim—was not lacking in either knowledge or method; however, it seems to have nothing to say about the political events which it disdained, those political events which the Russian Revolution had glaringly shown determined the fate of men. And now, here was Raymond Aron in Germany who would read a good number of authors who, to differing degrees, asked the same questions as the questions which the French ignored: what does it mean to understand a historic event? Can the historian achieve objectivity? What method is adapted to the understanding of the political and historical universe? What is the relationship between the actor and the spectator in history? Wilhelm Dilthey and Max Weber were the two greatest thinkers to deal with these questions.

Aron was above all fascinated by Weber. Above and beyond his incomparable erudition, his penetrating historical insights, the fecundity of his methodological propositions, the *Stimmung* of the German sociologist won him over: the existence simultaneously of the most rigorous scientific ideal and the most acute awareness of the tragic nature of history, tragic because it obliged human liberty to choose between causes when reason itself could not. Weber's influence on Aron, regularly remarked upon by commentators and recognized by Aron himself, is all the more worthy of our consideration precisely since the general tone of the two works is so different. Weber's vehement and movingly overcharged writing contrasts with Aron's extreme sobriety of tone. The latter never adopted in either style or thought the Nietzschean mood that was so evident in the work of the German sociologist. If Aron never systematically developed his criticism of the Weberian philosophy or method,[1] this criticism can be found and is nonetheless clear for its being implicit, in this stylistic difference: if, in order to remain faithful to the scientific ideal, we must renounce transcendental religions, then why conserve the pathos with which for ages the faithful described "the misery of man without God"? If scientific knowledge is today our only recourse, then why highlight the contradictions of life and science, dramatization which can only hinder the salutary influence of this knowledge upon action?

In any case, if this reception, renewal and correction of Max Weber had decisive consequences on Aron's own itinerary, its consequences on the destiny of Weber's thought were also not negligible. It was largely due to Aron that readers were prevented from becoming obsessed by Weberian Nietzscheism and expressionism, and that the knowledgeable and perceptive sociologist was not eclipsed by the *Machtpolitiker*. In some way, it is in part thanks to the Aronian renewal—Aron's interpretation of Weber as well as Aron's own personal work—that Max Weber owes his healthiest posterity in European sociology.

Indelibly marked by his encounter with Max Weber, Raymond Aron, back in France, wrote his "thèse d'État," which he defended in 1938 and published the same year under the title *Introduction à la Philosophie de l'Histoire*. The occasion was an intellectual event; the *Revue de Métaphysique et de Morale* gave an account of the defense.

Henri-Irénée Marrou said later that Aron's stay in Germany was an important moment for French intellectual history because it contributed substantially, by the intermediary of the dissertation, to the weakening of the then dominant historical and sociological positivism. Besides, the members of the jury—in particular the philosopher Leon Brunschvicg and the sociologists Célistin Bouglé and Paul Fauconnet—were themselves in one form or another, marked by this positivism. Therefore, while admiring Aron's intellectual performance, they remained uncertain—uncomfortable would perhaps be the better word—with regard to the implications and the significance of the Aronian thesis.

Perhaps the tone of this work—its "pathos" as Aron would refer to it later on with some severity—was influenced by the proximity of the war, the threat of which had been looming since 1933. A few months after the defense of his dissertation, the war broke out. After the defeat, Aron reached London and joined up with the Free French Forces. For four years he was editor in chief of the magazine *La France Libre*. Although he participated in this way in the effort to keep French culture alive outside of France, he refused to approve all facets of General de Gaulle's policy and in particular his claim to being the sole incarnation of national legitimacy. At least up until the Anglo-American debarkation in North Africa he regretted that Gaullist propaganda indiscriminately labeled traitor everyone who obeyed Marshal Pétain. He also regretted that for the head of Free France the intransigent affirmation of French identity and independence—as necessary as it was—required excessively aggressive behavior with regard to our allies. It is from this period on that the convictions—both moral and political—that were to govern Aron's political conduct and writings after the war appear: his reticence with regard to all behavior that tends to increase divisions between French men and women, divisions to which the French themselves are only too prone; a rejection of partisan propagandists who pretend to have a monopoly over patriotism; a reserve with regard to those political procedures inspired by XIXth century national or nationalistic *Machtpolitik*, a reserve tempered by the still acute awareness that questions of power and diplomatic independence are always essential to the life of a nation.

After the war, Raymond Aron went back to France and turned to journalism, refusing the sociology chair offered him by the University of Bordeaux. He was an editorialist at *Combat* (1946–1947), then at the *Figaro* (he was to remain there for thirty years, until 1977). In 1946 his friendly relations with Jean-Paul Sartre were broken off for political reasons, Sartre tending to become more and more a communist "fellow-traveler," while Aron became the sharpest critic of the

Soviet regime and of the favor or at least indulgence with which many intellectuals treated it. He developed his arguments on the subject in *Opium of the Intellectuals* (1955). His well-argued criticism of "sacred words" or of "myths"—Left, Revolution, Proletariat—his detailed analysis and comparison of the status of intellectuals in modern societies and the peculiarities of their history in France, make this book one of the most significant political works that have appeared in France and in Europe since the war. His main target was not so much the communists, who refused on principle, any debate with the "bourgeoisie," as the "progressives." The "progressives" were at the time full of severity for the least defects of the Western democracies and mobilized all their resources of subtlety to throw a veil over the worst crimes of the communists, in order to maintain the myth that despite everything the proletariat was destined to regenerate our old societies, and finally to establish the recognition of all for one and one for all. In fact, even in this book, Aron was less concerned with attacking the ideals of the left (which were and have remained his own to a certain degree) as their perversion. He analyzes how noble ideals have become destructive myths, by virtue of what ignorance, mental confusions, emotional thinking, such highly gifted minds as Sartre and Merleau-Ponty were capable—at least for a time—of making themselves the spokesmen for such a summary pro-communism, albeit draped and variegated in a Hegelian *trompe l'oeil*.

That same year, 1955, without giving up journalism, Raymond Aron took up his university career again. He was elected to the sociology chair of the Sorbonne. His courses, soon published, were rapidly considered classics of contemporary sociology: *Eighteen Lectures on Industrial Society* (1967); *La lutte de classes* (1964); *Democracy and Totalitarianism* (1965); *Main Currents in Sociological Thought* (1968 and 1970). This last work, a series of historical and intellectual portraits of the great figures of sociology—Montesquieu, Comte, Marx, Tocqueville, Durkheim, Pareto, Weber—played a particularly important role in expanding the memory of French sociologists. The Comtean-Durkheimian tradition—full of merits but also limits due above all to its disdain for the political field—is stripped of its founder's monopoly. At the two chronological extremes, the chapters on Montesquieu and Weber link the sociological point of view with the philosophical. At the center, the chapter on Tocqueville which rehabilitates or rather establishes the French politician as a first rank sociologist, demonstrates that the sociological point of view in no way necessarily prevents an attentive consideration of political phenomena, or conversely, that the belief that political phenomena are of decisive importance does not oblige one to renounce established sociological truths. The chapter of *Main Currents in Sociological Thought* devoted to Tocqueville, in addition to the analyses devoted two years earlier to the Tocquevillian conception of liberty in *Essai sur les libertés* (1965) played an important part in the rediscovery of the importance of Tocqueville for the understanding of democratic societies.

Then, toward the end of the '60s, when opinion and society seemed to be heading in the direction of "an end to ideologies," at least toward an appeasement of ideological tensions, and when Raymond Aron was on the verge of receiving in France the recognition that he had never lacked in the Anglo-Saxon world or in Germany, the "events of May '68" forced him on the opposite side of what was then the dominant opinion in French intellectual circles. In *The Elusive Revolution* (1969), he sharply attacked the student revolt. He who had been one of the French University's keenest critics found himself its most eloquent defender, faced with reformers whose slogans—No to selection, Student participation on exam juries, etc.—seemed to him to mean the end of any authentic university. More generally, Raymond Aron was repelled by the circus atmosphere of May '68, and also by its imitative quality: Paris tearing up its cobblestones was a replay of the great scenes of the XIX century, that of 1830 or 1848, without the excuse of misery or of an oppressive regime. Aron's very strong reaction to the events of '68 surprised, irritated, sometimes upset academics and intellectuals who were close to him in France or abroad. Perhaps it discouraged him to see that France, finally endowed since 1958 with solid institutions and having finally succeeded in modernizing its economy, therefore having overcome, it seemed, its main handicaps, was still so fragile that a few student riots could unleash a major crisis such as would endanger the republic itself. The threat that a Cohn-Bendit could overthrow General deGaulle incurred the wrath of Aron. Those whose serenity was not troubled by this perspective, those who were even enthusiastic at the idea may doubtlessly reproach him. We shall not forget, however, that according to classical philosophy, anger duly tempered by reason is a passion becoming the good citizen.

After 1968, we are witness to a bitter reideologization of some French intellectuals: dogmatic Marxist-Leninism inspired by the teachings and works of Louis Althusser saw its apogee. Aron wrote *D'une sainte famille à l'autre: Essai sur les marxismes imaginaire* (1969), in opposition to the latter and also to criticize Sartre whose "group in fusion" described in *Critique de la raison dialectique* had found some following in the fervor of the events. Curiously enough, we can date the end of the great ideological debate in France to this book. Of course not that this powerfully and brilliantly argued work had convinced his adversaries or even that the latter had bothered to discuss it. But it is the last time that an important text took note of the polarization of the French intellectual community into two irreconcilable camps, not only on the basis of a profound political disagreement but even more because their intellectual approaches were themselves incompatible. To be more precise, it is the last time that Aron would try in a critical fashion to enable these two different worlds to communicate with each other (for thirty years he was virtually the only one to try to fulfill this task of intellectual clarity and civic conversation). In the years that followed, the Marxist-Leninist camp of the top intelligentsia fell apart. For thirty years Aron had made his objections and offered his arguments with no other response most of the time than silent disdain or vehement invective. At the close of the battle, the adversary abandoned everything, arms and baggage; he would shortly reproach Raymond Aron with having spent too long a time stating the obvious. It was a famous victory.

After 1969, leaving all polemics aside, Raymond Aron undertook a major work on the strategic thought of Clausewitz and on his posthumous destiny. It was in 1976 that he published the two volumes of his monumental *Penser la guerre, Clausewitz*, that is generally considered his masterpiece. In 1970 he had been elected Professor at the Collège de France from which he retired in 1979. From 1977 until his death in October 1983 he was the President of the Editorial Committee of the weekly magazine *L'Express*.

The Philosopher

This brief biographical outline suggests the variety and amplitude of Raymond Aron's accomplishments. Few men of this century have been able like him to overcome the institutional conditions and the prevalent ways of thinking which almost inevitably push academics and scientists toward specialization. He can be equally felicitous and equally authoritative whether speaking with the philosopher or the statesman, the strategist or the economist. Nothing is as necessary to the vitality and even the survival of the public spirit in modern societies as the presence in their midst of such whole men. They ensure the communication between the different ruling elements or authorized groups which, each according to its own goals and methods, orient the fate of the political body. It is on this condition alone that democracies can mitigate the disintegrating effects of the excessive division of labor; on this condition alone that the art of politics can maintain its primary architectonic role.

When the same mind is capable of such varied accomplishments, one question naturally arises: do the different facets of his activity—philosophy, international relations, strategy, sociology, journalism—represent expressions of what is basically one world conception? Or, to be more precise, if we consider the intellectual biography of Raymond Aron, what is the meaning of his break with pure philosophy which comes after World War II?

We must keep in mind the subtitle of his 1938 thesis: *An Essay on the Limits of Historical Objectivity.* This work is a detailed study of the historic condition of man. The procedure is analytic. Aron does not describe the historic condition of man as the original event starting with and in the light of which everything that makes man should be understood. He doesn't seek to penetrate as such the enigmatic relationship that links man's humanity to Being and the question of Being to that of Time as Heidegger attempted to do in *Being and Time.* He describes, classifies and articulates the various fields of human existence in which man finds himself by his essence in direct or indirect relation with Time; so he surveys the several modes by which Time is experienced and known: from the knowledge of oneself to knowledge of others, from the various spiritual universes in which the individual has his place to the plurality of perspectives which are offered to him, as actor and as spectator, as private man, citizen, or historian. It is in order to be faithful to this plurality of human historicity that Aron sharply criticizes the two great strategies that have been adopted in modern times to neutralize the awareness of the paradoxes of historicity: on the one hand evolutionary determinism, and on the other, historical relativism. These two great types of doctrine appear to contradict each other: the first makes man the lord of time thanks to knowledge; the second makes him the plaything of time, by subordinating human experience and knowledge to the constantly new and unpredictable dispensations brought on or rendered possible by circumstances of time and place. In fact, both equally eliminate the unique character of man's historic condition and its specific tragedy which resides precisely in the fact that man is neither the master nor the plaything of time. Therefore Aron tries to maintain the heterogeneity of the fields of Being and of the spiritual universes: each one must be taken on its own terms. For example, time, which is a succession of living species in the various theories of evolution cannot be thought of in the same breath as truly historic time in which man accomplishes his deeds and creates his works. Similarly Aron upholds philosophy's claim that it cannot legitimately be deduced from something other than itself, which "in the last analysis" would have a molding or determining effect upon it: history, whether it refers specifically to "history of the relations of production" or "history of civilization" or "history of science" cannot be a substitute for philosophy. The following quote indicates Aron's basic thinking on this matter, with its ambiguity: "The possibility of a philosophy of history finally merges with the possibility of a philosophy in spite of history. . . ." Such a formula characteristically ignores a third possibility, the Hegelian possibility, that the culmination of history and the culmination of philosophy are one and the same, and thus that *all* history can be reconciled with *all* philosophy. In fact, Hegel is almost absent from this book (or he is present only through Marx's mediation), while Rickert, Simmel, Weber, Bergson, and Comte are analyzed, often in detail. History and Philosophy therefore in Aron's thesis have a relationship that is at once ambiguous, novel and enigmatic; this is the most important point to clarify if we are to understand the later works of Aron.

One might perhaps state the following: Aron's thesis gives too much weight to historicism—to the idea that man is essentially a historic being who fashions himself and determines himself within history—to admit as classical philosophy did a theory of man's nature and condition *sub specie aeternitatis*; on the other hand, it retains too much of the traditional conception of philosophy—as the elaboration of universal articulations of the human experience—to succumb to the seduction of either relativism or of the historic totality, Hegelian or Marxist. Aron, while refusing both a philosophy which would abolish history and a theory of history which would abolish philosophy, tries to delimit and mark the intermediary terrain defined by the insurmountable distance between philosophy and history. Herein lies that which one might call his Kantianism: indeed, reason provides us with "regulatory ideas" to orient us within history and in one way to judge history; however, even if one is allowed to hope that humanity will in the future conform more readily to the requirements of reason, we cannot conceive of history as being the history of the triumph of reason. Between the universal which concerns philosophy and the particular in which real man is immersed, stretches a territory that one might call philosophically neutral. The Aronian attitude is best defined perhaps by the refusal to succumb to two spells: on the one hand, the spell of the philosophic quest which aims for the universal, to attain the Unconditioned; on the other, the spell of historic idolatry which sees in a particular people or class or historic moment the incarnation of the universal.

We will limit ourselves to one remark, suggested by the comments of Gaston Fessard, on the difficulty of maintaining oneself on this neutral territory. In a striking passage from his thesis, Raymond Aron writes that there is no history of religion either for the believer or for the unbeliever: for the believer who by an act of faith adheres to the eternal, there is no history; for the unbeliever, there is no transcendent order. This perceptive remark certainly points to one of the major difficulties of that which we call the "social sciences." However, to confine oneself to this alternative without taking sides for one or the other of the terms, or without suggesting a procedure that would enable one eventually to overcome or to circumvent this alternative, Aron's critical philosophy of history seems condemned to say nothing concerning the great religious phenomena which have contributed in such a large way to the fashioning of our history. Might the critical philosophy of history, by methodological rigor, necessarily tend to dissolve the very subject matter of its inquiry?

Raymond Aron would answer probably that this objection does not take sufficiently into account the limits of reason, "the limits of historical objectivity": if reason can say nothing concerning the truth—total, partial or non-existent—of such revealed religion, for example, the philosopher can but take note of this fact; but this negative acknowledgment is nevertheless not empty or sterile since therein we can see one of the contradictions inherent in the human condition, that between reason and revelation. It would only be empty and sterile if we conceive of reason as a faculty or power which would by right extend its jurisdiction over the totality of the natural and human world: in this case, indeed, the incapacity of reason to tell us anything about religious phenomena as such would be a radical failure which would shed doubt upon the definition of man as a rational animal. But if reason is conceived of as a *human* faculty, that is to say *finite*, incapable of giving us access to the ultimate cause of things or of enabling us to seize the totality of history, then the recognition of its limits in no way takes away from its authority *within* those limits: to live according to reason remains the specifically and eminently human task, that in which man recognizes simultaneously his excellence and his finiteness.

These remarks help us to understand why, in the later career of Raymond Aron, philosophy in the more restricted and academic sense of the term gets relegated to the background. Events, institutions, societies must be confronted and understood on their own terms and not on the basis of a philosophy of history, which, exceeding the limits of reason, would eliminate their contingency and dissolve their individuality. To understand events on their own terms is to understand the intentions and the deeds of the historic actors; and one cannot understand these intentions and deeds unless we envisage them first of all as the actors themselves have done. There is a density and an intelligibility inherent in historic events that the interpreter, philosopher or historian cannot reduce to a set of historic or sociological "laws" without annulling precisely this particular density and intelligibility. The historian's interest in a particular event or period—interest determined or influenced from the start by a multitude of factors: a certain something in the air, one's own personal political passions, scientific ideal . . .—is made possible by the interest that the actors themselves have shown in the events. This is why historical narrative, such as the finished model that Thucydides left us holds an irreducible validity and dignity for Aron: "The passage from the individual act to the supra-individual event is accomplished through the narrative, without breaking the continuity, without substituting general propositions to the reconstitution of the facts, by the sole confrontation of what the actors wanted and actually happened" (*Thucydide et le récit historique*, in *Dimensions de la conscience historique*, 1961). The intelligibility of history is first of all the intelligibility of the actions of the actors. The reflection on the Thucydidean narrative serves as the link in Aron's development between the critique of historical reason on the one hand, and the analysis of strategic problems and commentary upon events on the other.

Aron's philosophic work as such has not received, at least until recent years, the attention that it merits. For France, the reasons are easy to comprehend. The long rupture caused by the war and by the occupation had dislocated intellectual customs and communications. Minds eager for a future that would in no way resemble the past, turned away from the works and men of the pre-war period: we have only to think of Bergson's near-disappearance from the French consciousness after 1945. Aron himself confirmed this break by not returning to the University and by adopting a mode of expression, journalism, quite distant from the philosophic genre; more important still, Aron most often does not relate even his non-journalistic post-war works to his previous philosophic reflection. Finally, it must be said, without presuming to pass judgment on the authors that benefited from it, that French philosophy entered into a period where fashion, stardom and confusion between philosophic rigor and literary amenities seriously compromised its working conditions. Merleau-Ponty and above all Sartre were the main beneficiaries of this state of mind. Of course, it was legitimate that the merits of Sartre as a writer, as a psychologist, and as a philosopher were generally recognized. But one cannot help but think that in the person of Sartre, France, perhaps for the last time, offered itself the royal luxury of having a favorite, something it had since the XVIIIth century loved to offer itself.

Actually, between *Being and Nothingness* and *The Introduction to the Philosophy of History*, there were numerous affinities, due to the common philosophic training of the two authors, due also to their conversations at the École Normale. If Sartre's book was more directed at one's sensitivity and imagination, if it had a more moving eloquence, Aron's book was more rigorous, more balanced, and above all lent itself to developments and in-depth studies that the Sartrian mode of expression, always peremptory, always definitive, always absolute, forbade. However that may be, Raymond Aron had to pay this price—to renounce his philosophic work already in progress—in order to become what he was, in order that past philosophic works and the possible philosophic work—the possible is not the unreal—be refracted in a thousand elusive but effective ways in his understanding. This, in order that one of the most intelligent young men that had become that which French culture, which is not a civic culture, does not willingly produce and recognizes with great reticence, that is to say, a public man who speaks with authority and competence about matters of the city, a man whose eloquence is capable of teaching the public as it is of holding the ear of Princes and Consuls, a man whose sovereign reason captures the essence of each situation, in order that he become that which the Romans called—a word whose full measure we no longer comprehend—an *orator*.

The Strategist

It is perhaps in his works on strategic problems and on war that the first philosophic research by Aron found its most explicit and fecund refraction. War is diametrically opposed to the moral imperative of the Kantian philosopher, and at the same time, it can in no way be ignored by the political thinker. The *ought* and the *is* are here clearly and cruelly differentiated by reality itself. Moreover, it is in the strategic decisions that the role of actor and the role of reason in the deeds of this actor are given center stage. The approach of a strategist is or wishes to be purely rational, while the outcome of this approach is fundamentally uncertain. This high exercise of reason is not a science; the "limits of historic objectivity" are the very condition for action and dictate its urgency. The undertaking which fascinates Aron is precisely to try to reach this extreme and paradoxical point where reason is at its highest degree of power and at the same time fragility.

By his essays devoted to the problems of nuclear strategy, *The Century of Total War* (1954) and *The Great Debate* (1963), Raymond Aron initiated his readers—and perhaps military and political leaders—to the niceties and paradoxes of the American theories of deterrence. But perhaps unlike many authors of strategy, he has always been particularly sensitive to the extremely abstract nature of these theories, to their dependence upon summary and questionable psychological hypotheses and to general political conditions as well. From his first strategic essays, and even before having delved into the study of Clausewitz, Aron always underlined the importance of political matters in the elaboration of a judicious strategic discourse.

Peace and War (1966) is a general survey, which tries to situate the problems of war, peace and strategy in a theory of international relations. But Aron, always acutely aware of the irreducible nature of action, notices that there cannot be a general theory of international relations comparable to the general theory of economy. In this work, full of historical examples, he analyzes the meaning of diplomatic conduct, brings out fundamental notions, specifies the variables which one must examine in order to understand a diplomatic constellation. He does not try to construct a closed system.

If *Penser la guerre, Clausewitz* is generally considered Raymond Aron's masterpiece, it is no doubt because the work is an expression of his diverse intellectual and human interests. First of all, the profound familiarity and love of Aron for the German language and culture. One of the tasks to which he dedicated himself was the bringing together of France and Germany. What could be more paradoxically moving than this encounter with the enemy of Napoleon, who hated the French, and who nevertheless knew how to silence his prejudices and passions when it was a question of understanding and of making understood the strategic genius of Napoleon, the "god of war"? In one sense isn't Aron to Clausewitz what Clausewitz is to Napoleon? How can one not be but touched by the personality of this period as well? Brutal of course—and preparing by its mass mobilizations for the total wars of the XXth century—but still conserving, even in the relationships between enemies, a humanity which will be lost in our century? One of Clausewitz's moving charms, as Aron recreates him, is to have combined the coldest realism with the élans and enthusiasm of German idealism. Aron, who of all authors is the least disposed to nostalgia, paints this period not only knowledgeably but *con amore*: one could legitimately say *Das ist ein Mensch* of many great

actors and in every camp. All his readers have noted with what respect, with what affectionate delicacy Aron painted the portrait of the
Prussian general, emphasizing the tormented aspect of his soul: living
amidst the aristocracy but in a precarious situation, esteemed but not
recognized for his true merits, ambitious and oversensitive, always
carrying with him the unrealized desire for a more brilliant destiny.
Throughout his analysis of the greatest strategic author, Aron brings
to life the human qualities of these imperious and tender souls; in his
meditations upon the first great modern European war, Aron has
brought his own humanity to bear: grasping the most sensitive point,
the sorest point of the common history of these two countries when
the logic of hatred which would humiliate both of them each in its
turn is set off, he has enlarged the common memory of France and of
Germany; he has enriched and humanized the memory of Europe.

In the speculative field, that which interests Aron is the theory of
action, of which military action is but an eminent example. How to
think action which is itself incertitude? How to *think* that which is
not real but possible because it depends upon human choice? Returning to the problem of the *Introduction* and of his work on Max Weber,
he asks himself what kind of theory will enable us to understand and
shed light upon action without falling into doctrinairism which dissolves the incertitude and therefore the liberty of action in a false
necessity or rationality but without admitting either that the world of
action is pure confusion unamenable to reason. Just as in the *Introduction* Aron looks for a via media between evolutionary dogmatism
and historicist relativism, in *Clausewitz* he searches for a *via media*
between doctrinairism and empiricism; in short, he wishes to recon-
quer the field of practical philosophy or of practical reason, not by a
return to the Aristotelian doctrine but by using the conceptual tools
forged by those authors whom we might situate on the frontier between philosophy and social science, such as Montesquieu or Max
Weber.

Perhaps the work on Clausewitz allows us to understand why Aron
did not write the book on Machiavelli which he had intended to write
for a long time, nor the synthesis on Marx that has been asked of him
for a generation, nor has he followed up the parallel between Machiavelli and Marx that he, himself, sketched out. Between the Italian
patriot who exalts the founding prince, ex nihilo, of the *ordini nuovi*
and the German doctrinairian who with jubilant indignation unravels
cruel historic necessity, Clausewitz embodies the golden mean capable of harmonizing judiciously constraints and liberty of action. The
"strange trinity" of war according to Clausewitz—the People's passions, the free activity of the soul of the war Chief, the sovereign and

regulatory understanding of the political Chief—is this not the emblem of man's political condition, of the conditions for human action in the political world?

Aron establishes with faultless erudition how Clausewitz, far from being the prophet of absolute war, of the rise to extremes, of the militarization of politics is, on the contrary, always careful to show that military objectives—victory first of all—only have meaning in relation to political goals; he shows in particular that this is the sense of the all-too-famous formula: "War is the continuation of politics by other means," a formula so often interpreted the other way round. The idea of absolute war, the rise to extremes, the unconditional victory belong to the *concept* of war as a duel of wills, but this concept of war does not presume to reflect reality nor still less tell us what war should be; it condenses the logic implicit in all war, logic which is modified, sometimes considerably, by the circumstances, and more essentially by the influence of political objectives, by the rationality of political understanding.

The second volume of *Clausewitz* is composed of two parts. The first part—"Prosecutor or defendant?"—is an interrogation on the destiny and posthumous influence of Clausewitz. In particular Aron examines the influence of his teachings on the Schlieffen Plan and on the military leaders of World War I such as Foch or Ludendorff; he then considers the use to which Lenin and later Mao Zedong put Clausewitz's Treatise. To different degrees and for sometimes opposite reasons, all these men more or less misunderstood Clausewitz rather than enriched him. The fresco painted by Aron offers us the dismemberment of the Prussian strategist's "trinity": while Western doctrine and military practice give precedence to freedom of activity of the war Chief, Maoist ideology and practice emphasize the People, while the Soviets tend to accentuate unilaterally the primacy of understanding and of political objectives. In spite of its unilateral nature and ideological trappings which have nothing to do with Clausewitz's thinking, the Soviet strategic doctrine retains with good sense in any case a central aspect of the Treatise, which Westerners have a tendency to forget. The elaboration of Clausewitz's true thinking enables Aron to reclaim our true possession from the Soviets, a balanced strategic doctrine which they engross, mutilate and use to their own ends.

The second part of the second volume—"The Nuclear Age, The Wager with Reason"—is an analysis of international relations in the nuclear age, an in-depth reflection, nourished by events, on the problems of deterrence, the wars of national liberation, the new nature of revolutionary violence. Throughout this part, Aron shows himself to be very sensitive to a radical difference which distinguishes strategic reflection after Hiroshima from strategic reflection in the time of Clausewitz. The Napoleonic wars, however bloody they were, did not however undo the fabric of common humanity. The threat of nuclear annihilation abolishes that part of humanity which in those days remained in reflections upon war and in war itself: "Today whoever contemplates wars and strategy raises a barrier between his intelligence and his humanity."

And yet, in this book, and this is perhaps its greatest virtue as a book to educate, the reader always encounters intelligence and humanity together. But humanity is present—as it is in all of Aron's work—with a sobriety, a reserve which sometimes renders it imperceptible to our contemporaries, used as they are to the stridency of fine sentiments. This is why, reading Aron, the reader will recall more than once Thucydides whose tranquil courage, free as he was of illusion, always discerns in the most inhuman constraints the play of liberty, the human element.

The Sociologist

The sociological analyses of Raymond Aron have become part of our pluralistic societies' awareness of themselves. He is reproached, in France particularly, with being essentially critical, in such a way that he would leave us without guidelines, without landmarks to help us construct a better society. In fact, in conformity with the neutral philosophic position that was described above, Aron at no moment offers us a model for the good society or for the best regime. Nor does he offer a doctrine describing and elaborating the principles according to which the good society should be constructed and with reference to which consequently all existing societies could and should be judged. Aron's point of departure is what our societies say about themselves, the ideals which they profess, principally liberty and equality. Then he analyzes the meaning or meanings of each of these ideals and how these ideals may agree or conflict, in which context their conflict is inevitable. One will find a remarkable example of this procedure in *An Essay on Freedom* (1970). Such a procedure is necessary according to him in order to understand the societies in which we live; moreover, it moderates the exaggerated hopes born of the illusion of being able to multiply in all circumstances the advantages of liberty by those of equality. One must beware of this illusion because it risks causing undertakings which endanger both liberty and equality. More basically, if we keep in mind his Kantian background, we can say that this type of analysis is an inquiry into the antinomies of the human condition.

Assuredly, Aron never questions the ultimate value of these ideals themselves; more generally, he never questions the ultimate value of modern ideals (which include not only equality and liberty, but also, for example, technical progress and industrialization). But by virtue of his philosophic point of view it cannot be otherwise: if he does not believe that the history of the world is the "tribunal of the world," neither does he think that it is possible to find an ultimate criterion for judgment outside of or above history, unless it be in the moral conscience of the individual who, in a given situation, can, and sometimes must, prefer what ought to be to what is. In certain circumstances, one can but say—it is an expression that Aron loves to quote—as Luther said to the Diet of Worms: *Hier stehe ich; ich kann nicht anders.* But this contingent encounter between a situation and a duty cannot be formalized and generalized into a doctrine of the True and the Good which would, so to speak, bypass the contingencies and the constraints of history.

The advantages of such a philosophic position can be seen in the works that Aron devoted to modern societies and political regimes: *Eighteen Lectures on Industrial Society; La lutte de classes; Democracy and Totalitarianism.* That which the public has above all retained from these books is the importance Aron gives to the notion of *industrial society.* This notion englobes as one genre two political species: liberal-capitalist regimes on the one hand, and totalitarian-communist regimes on the other. On both sides of the Iron Curtain, Aron sees the same constraints imposed and the same aspirations expressed: the scientific organization of work, the necessity to invest, the desire to increase productivity, etc. Beyond Marx, he renews with the Saint-Simonian vision: modern societies are specifically characterized by the application of science to the exploitation of nature, by industrialism. Accordingly, at least in the *Eighteen Lectures*, Aron tended to relegate to the background the importance of political regimes, the radicality of the difference between the liberal regime, which he readily calls constitutional-pluralist, and the communist regime. This is at least the reproach made of him by some. It is certainly true that he never preached the doctrine of the "convergence" between East and West, but it is also true that his insistence on the characteristics common to all industrial societies seems to be out of kilter with regard to the never belied intransigence of his opposition to communism.

In fact, we must distinguish two elements in this emphasis upon the notion of industrial society. We have already mentioned the first, which is Aron's Saint-Simonism; furthermore, one must add that Aron, who had observed with consternation the disasters of France's economic policy between the two wars, was greatly and happily impressed by the impetuous post-war growth and therefore by this very fact spontaneously open to the influence of the "theories of growth," in particular that of Colin Clark. In the Aronian notion of "industrial society," the neutral judgment—the specific feature of modern society is industrialism—is to a certain extent reenforced and kindled by Aron's choice in favor of industry and economic growth.

But the notion of industrial society plays another role in Aron's approach. Since precisely it is indisputable that industry is one of the points in common between Western societies and those of the East, then to insist on this fact is to assert that a comparative discourse is both possible and reasonable; it is to make a direct attack upon the communist dogma concerning the incommensurability of the two types of societies (dogma which underlies and conditions that of the superiority of communist societies). To elaborate the notion of industrial society was not to announce the "convergence"; nor was it even to attempt to initiate a dialogue with the communists who in any case would not have been open to one; it was rather to suggest a language and notions which could in France but also in other Western nations, reestablish the communication between anti-communist liberals and the Marxist-leaning or industrialist Left who no longer believed in the official version of communist society but who were not yet ready to see the whole reality. In fact, it is indeed thus that, for the essentials, the notion of industrial society played its role in the public consciousness: it served less to reconcile liberals with communism than certain disillusioned communists or Marxists with capitalism. It is not only by his polemics, but also by the irenical concept of industrial society that Raymond Aron has contributed to maintaining intellectual communication between the two camps which divided the French conscience.

The basic problem remains: does the notion of industrial society blur the specificity of the communist regime? The answer to this question can only be positive. But Aron's position on this point is somewhat paradoxical: often—taking up, deliberately or not, the classical tradition—he underlines the decisive importance of the political regime in the conformation of a society and characterizes the communist regime as *ideocracy*; this is what he does in *Democracy and Totalitarianism*; it explains more generally his predilection for the more politically attuned sociologists such as Montesquieu or Tocqueville.

Doubtless there is in Aron's thinking a tension between the economist or the Saint-Simonian and the political liberal, tension which perhaps echoes that between the sociologist and the philosopher. From the opposite point of view, one might consider that in him two traditions which when they were not ignoring each other were fighting each other find reconciliation, traditions whose meeting in reality if not in people's minds—the joining of industrial organization and political liberties—defines the nature of modern Western society.

The preceding remarks should in no case obscure a central feature of the significance of the work and the activity of Aron: since the end of the last war he has been one of the most steadfast, most intransigent, most enlightened adversaries of communism. His understanding of the absolutely deadly character of the threat of communism which hangs over civilization and humanity, was immediate and total, free of those hesitations and those mental reservations which have for such a long time paralyzed so many intelligent minds. If knowing how to identify the enemy—who he is and what he is—is the most eminent *political virtue*, Aron possesses this virtue to the highest degree. And in the case of communism, which aims to destroy not only democracy but the elementary conditions for a truly human life, the judgment concerning the enemy is more and better than a simple political judgment, it is a judgment that is inseparably political and spiritual. In his combat against communism, Raymond Aron is inseparably *defensor civitatis* and *defensor humanitatis*.

The Educator

Raymond Aron's role as political commentator represents a highly unusual situation, at least in France. Montesquieu remarks that in free regimes, if the historian is at his leisure to look for and to pronounce the truth, he rarely uses this opportunity since he is so busy maintaining the prejudices of the factions, those factions which are inseparable from liberty. What Montesquieu says about historians is even more true of journalists or of political commentators. In order to know what they are going to say, it usually suffices to know if they belong to the majority or to the opposition party. Aron has never been a partisan journalist. When the right was in power and he was one of the most scathing critics of the left within the intellectual community, he was never "governmental": when he esteemed that the government has committed an error, he said so and argued his point of view. It is thus that the first three Presidents of the Fifth Republic discovered that they could not "count on him." It is precisely for this reason that the public debate owes Aron so much. One trait of his journalistic style must be mentioned here: its enlightening terseness. Aron the journalist has the incomparable art of pointing out in a few words—without invective, without malicious personal attack, without pathos—the weakness in the armor, be it the imprudence of some diplomatic step, the absurdity of an economic choice or simply the vacuity of a speech. In the never-ending confusion of the political debate of a democratic nation in love with words, he has the perspicacity of one whom Erasmus emblematically calls "the night hawk," "who sees very clearly in the midst of darkness." It is for this reason that for over thirty years Aron's formulas circulate so often in political conversations in France.

Journalism: on this point so apparently far from philosophy in Aron's career, we must halt for an instant. It seems to me that the role that the political Aron has in relation to Aron the philosopher, the Kantian Aron, is analogous to that which the political Cicero had with Cicero the philosopher: the orator knows that the stars exist, but most often he leaves it to the others to describe the movement of the constellations; or, if he ventures therein himself sometimes, his voice betrays a saddened irony. His own task is to introduce a bit of order and clarity into the sublunar world: to do this one must forget the stars as much as one remembers them. One higher Reason and Justice preside perhaps, mysteriously, over the destinies of the world, however improbable that may be; but the task of human reason and justice is, given the constraints and the incertitudes of effective action, to limit the powers of the inhuman. In a way, Raymond Aron has never ceased to develop his thesis on the "limits of historic objectivity" in the most difficult manner that there is: by interpreting day after day history in the making.

At the beginning I said that Raymond Aron reconciled three fidelities: the fidelity to the German philosophic ambition, the fidelity to the French intransigence and clarity, and the fidelity to Anglo-Saxon civism. Without boastfulness or pomposity, he is what Nietzsche asked us to be: a "good European." Aron upheld with all his force every initiative in the direction of an institutionalized Europe; but at least as important as the institutions is the European spirit. The history of each European nation is too long and too particular for the European spirit to be anything in the foreseeable future other than the spirit of the European nations: it can only be crystallized therefore by the efforts of individuals who, belonging to one or another of these nations, nevertheless have an open enough mind to inherit, so to speak, the culture of other European nations. Any other unification of the European spirit would be artificial, at best impoverishing, at worst ideological. It is because Raymond Aron by so many traits is a French patriot that his contribution to the European spirit, to the communication between European nations and their memories, is so fecund.

Raymond Aron is a French patriot; he is a Jew, an assimilated Jew. Soberly assuming his Jewishness without affirming it aggressively, he has never considered that he belonged to two communities each of which required his allegiance. The only community which requires his allegiance is the French nation; to the Jewish people, to the State of Israel he feels bound by solidarity. His position has raised a lot of criticism, as any formulation of Jewishness necessarily must. Jews of the diaspora escape the accusation of betraying the Jewish people and the State of Israel. Even stronger, they are often faced simultaneously with these two accusations, as Aron has been. When a problem is theoretically insoluble, he who is faced with the problem must try not to render it even more insoluble: the consciousness of the depth of a problem is not measured by the stridency of the attitudes invoked.

Aron's reserve and sobriety also characterize his attitude with regard to Christianity, Catholicism in particular, so important in French history and conscience by the adhesions and the oppositions that it has raised. Raymond Aron is an unbeliever; not only is he an unbeliever but his writings do not betray that religious anxiety or that nostalgia for the ages of faith which one discerns in so many modern atheists, and which one encounters in Max Weber in particular. On the other hand, one never finds in Aron those moqueries or those points so characteristic of the tradition of the French Enlightenment to which he belongs. Has Aron attained that state which few Frenchmen, even today, know, that of "religious indifference"? We would be tempted to say he is insensitive to the religious tradition of Judaism because for him, for French culture, religion is identified with Christianity, and he is, however, indifferent to Christianity because he is Jewish. Perhaps this formula contains an element of truth. However, if in some mysterious way, our friends are a part of us and that which we are, then it is worth mentioning this: those minds which were the most spontaneously and most deeply attentive to the philosophical work of Aron were Catholics, in particular the historian Henri-Irénée Marrou and the Jesuit Father Gaston Fessard. That, as one says, proves nothing. It is true. But in Europe, in France in particular, "free-thinking" and the Catholic religion maintain complex, mysterious relations that the recognition of their opposition does not wear out: above and beyond this radical opposition which one does not have the right to attenuate, tacit complicities, unformulatable affinities paint, beneath the battlefield, the invisible network of a fraternity whose secret no one knows. The Catholic friendships which have surrounded and which surround Aron the agnostic or atheist are a sign of the unavowed part of the French soul.

Europe, since its origins—and this is what defines the "crisis" which is consubstantial with it—has been looking for the political regime in which it could finally settle happily and live normally. Since the end of the Roman Empire, it has never been able to obtain this so coveted benediction. For two centuries, this desire and this impulse have been pressing, devouring, frenetic. As Nietzsche says, the history of Europe makes one think today of a river which wants to "end things." To put an end to history, to put an end to wandering, such is the major temptation of the century, essentially in revolutionary undertakings but also in reactionary combats. This is why the principal virtue of political order, *prudence*, inseparable from *moderation,* is discredited to the extent that it is: it alone allows one to unite conservation to innovation and to creation; it alone guarantees the salutary influence of reason and protects us from the temptation of petrifying social life by imposing by means of violence "rational society," in fact, the enemy of all reason as of all humanity. In this century, Raymond Aron is an exemplary representative of this cardinal virtue. Without making himself the preacher of moderation, without making this virtue an explicit theme of his writings, he illustrates it in each one of his deeds and speeches. Formed of institutions whose different logics are often ill-assorted and sometimes contradictory, inheritor of inimical traditions, Europe's only chance to remain faithful to its plural essence is if the art of politics manages to weave together institutions, traditions, passions, virtues which, if each one were left to itself, would destroy the fragile equilibrium of European life. This is why Raymond Aron, intransigent adversary of communism, intransigent defender of liberal institutions, was never a doctrinaire liberal, a fanatic of the abstraction known as "the market." He never succumbed to the temptation which is, so to speak, consubstantial with political reflection, that of ideology. His analyses prolong and shed light upon the problems with which political actors, citizens or statesmen are actually confronted in the city; he in no way pretends to have access to a superior point of view which would allow him to neglect the weight of institutions, the logic of situations, the passions of the citizen, the incertitudes of the statesman.

A spectator and an actor in a period of European history in which thought has become its own enemy, in which certain of the greatest minds have consented—for a time or to the very end—to voluntary servitude, Raymond Aron has shown that the mind could be free in-history and in the city. Since he never believed that history was the realization of reason, he contributed to introducing a bit of reason into European politics; because he never believed that democratic man should be overcome and surpassed, but enlightened and encouraged, he contributed to introducing a bit of humanity into European democracy; because he never wished to reign in pride, he was never obliged to obey slavishly; he is a witness to the freedom of the spirit in history, an educator of the European city.

Notes

1. He has approached such a critique in the remarkable Introduction to *Le Savant et le politique* (Plon, 1959) (Note of Manent). See the English translation, "Max Weber and Social Science," in F. Draus, ed., *History, Truth, Liberty* (Chicago: University of Chicago Press, 1985), pp. 335–73.

Part One

**Beyond Weber and Machiavelli:
Toward a Morality of Prudence**

Introduction

Aron and Weber

> When I read Max Weber for the first time thirty years ago, I was particularly struck by the lesson of intellectual courage and modesty contained in his work. I still believe that his work contains a lesson which remains valid for us. But today I also realize that this thinking, which claims to be free of all illusion, stems from metaphysics, and a pessimistic vision of the world.
>
> — Raymond Aron, *Max Weber and Power-Politics*

Aron tells us in his autobiographical Inaugural Address at the Collège de France, "The Historical Condition of the Sociologist" (1970), that he was originally attracted to the work of Weber as an antidote to the naive optimism and literary politics of the dominant currents of French philosophic thought after World War I. The great events of the first part of the twentieth century, including a devastating world war and the rise of totalitarian regimes and secular religions in Russia, Italy, and Germany had not shaken French sociology and philosophy out of its dogmatic progressivist slumber. For Aron, confronting the rise of National Socialism in pre-Hitler Germany, the sociology of Max Weber seemed to be free of all progressivist illusions. Instead of a too facile faith in the inevitable march of reason and science, Weber's work presented a seemingly realistic and tragic "sociology of the war among classes, parties, and gods." Aron felt an almost immediate "elective affinity" with a thinker whose realism seemed able to account for the ideological storms unfolding before him in the Berlin of 1932 and 1933.

Aron, however, came to note the presence of quasi-nihilistic premises and a pessimistic distortion of reality behind what purported to be a realistic sociology of man and society. Aron's relationship with Weber after World War II is characterized by a recognition and rejection of Weber's pessimistic and irrationalist "metaphysics." Weber

asserted that there were two approaches to political "ethics": the ethicist of conviction, the revolutionary or pacificist, does what he will,
remains obstinately "committed" to his cause no matter what the consequences; the ethicist of responsibility recognizes a dialectic of means
and ends and concerns himself with the consequences of a political
action or choice. Aron often used this distinction and was attracted to
the *moderation* that seems inherent in an ethics of responsibility. But
Aron and Weber understood the ethics of reponsibility in decisively
different ways. Weber believed that all choices of values were idio-
syncratic and groundless. Reason cannot guide or moderate human and
political choice. "Men must choose their gods who may turn out to
be devils," as Weber argued in his famous essay, *Science as a Vocation*. Men choose their gods or demons and between such deities there
is relentless, *inexpiable* war. Aron recognized that human beings arrive at different representations of reality, that political life is often
characterized by a "war of the churches." But he opposed the trans-
formation of a sociological fact—the war of the churches—into a
dogmatic, pathetic philosophy, the *war of the gods*. For Aron, the
"ethics of responsibility," in a word political moderation and peace,
is more consistent with the nature and aspirations of human beings
and therefore rationally preferable to frenzied commitment and inexpiable war.

The first study in this section is a 1964 work entitled "Max Weber
and Power-Politics" delivered at the International Weber Conference
held in Heidelberg on the centenary of Weber's birth. This piece de-
lineates important differences between Aron's so-called realism and
Weber's philosophy of *Machtpolitik*. Weber was a partisan of the German Reich; he made a value choice for its power and power-prestige.
Every people and nation are members or ought to be members of a
unitary *culture*, a culture whose superiority or inferiority to other cultures is beyond the competency and capacity of reason to evaluate. A
nation characterized by a highly developed culture is a god or demon
to which men are irrationally but resolutely committed. The task of
statecraft is to maximize the power and power-prestige of one's *Kul-
tur*. No genuine cosmopolitan community of minds, nor transpolitical
recognition of shared principles, can overcome the *fact* that individuals and communities are ultimately at war. For Weber, "power-politics" is both a description of and a prescription for the behavior of
men and cities in a world of heterogenous and incompatible cultures,
nations, and ideologies.

To this Aron responds: yes, nations must look after themselves in
a world of conflicting regimes, parties, and principles. But this does

not mean that the fundamental spiritual fact about the human condition is war or that augmenting the power of one's people is the one and only imperative of international statecraft. The recognition of a common humanity and the refusal to do anything to other peoples in pursuit of one's national and foreign policy goals are also facts of social existence that citizens and statesmen must take into account. In *Peace and War* (1966) Aron advocates a morality of prudence which recognizes both the asocial *and* social dimensions of international relations. The citizens and statesmen guided by this morality try, not to establish perpetual peace, for that is an idealistic illusion which abstracts from the tragic dimension of the political situation of man, but to mitigate violence in the relations between states. For Aron the realist, in juxtaposition to Weber, the fundamental imperative guiding political man ought to be to maximize the presence of reason and moderation in a political world characterized by inevitable limitations and often difficult and contradictory choices. Aronian realism—because it recognizes the existence of cosmopolitan principles of reason, liberty, and right above and judging, however dimly, the patriotisms of different nations and cultures—has more in common with the hardheaded but liberal, politic, and cosmopolitan patriotism of Montesquieu and Tocqueville than the anguished and pathetic commitment of Weber to the power of the Reich. Aron, of course, recognized Weber's commitment to parliamentary and legal institutions and practices in Germany. He knew that Weber, a decent and civilized man, would have detested the brutality, vulgarity, and arbitrariness of Hitler and the National Socialists. But in completely jettisoning a foundation for his liberalism and parliamentarianism either in natural right or in a universal and rational vocation for man, Weber's thought, if not his practice, ultimately slides toward nihilism.

Max Weber and Power-Politics

Raymond Aron

1964

The task which you have entrusted to me has set me a problem of conscience, or, if I dare at this stage use an expression of Weber's, a problem of both science and politics. Max Weber, as we know, was not only the sociologist and philosopher whom we all admire, he was a political thinker, a publicist, who on several occasions thought of becoming a politician. Even if he never did enter active politics, he was nonetheless throughout his life the friend, counsellor and inspirer of men engaged in the day-to-day political struggle (e.g., Friedrich Naumann). I cannot therefore present or discuss certain of Weber's ideas and positions without suggesting judgments on Wilhelminian Germany or even German nationalism of that time, even if I do not formulate them in detail.

At another period in time, a Frenchman would have been able to refuse, and indeed ought to have refused, to write such a report: he would have been afraid of being tactless if he expressed himself frankly, and would have been less than frank if he had tried not to hurt any tender feelings. Personally I have not felt that I should be guided by such national considerations at this time and in these circumstances.

It is true that Max Weber does not belong to a past which is over and done with. The controversies aroused by W. Mommsen's book, *Max Weber und die deutsche Politik*,[1] are not purely scientific. They are also concerned with the significance we now attach to Wilhelminian Germany, to the First World War, to the Weimar Republic, and, by the same token, to Hitler and the Second World War. As a "power politician," Max Weber belongs to a past whose interpretation influences our awareness of the present situation. In this sense a Frenchman's participation in the discussion might appear indiscreet, if there were not three good reasons for waiving possible objections.

31

First of all, I am not personally suspected of being anti-Weber, even if I could no longer express myself today exactly as I did thirty years ago in the *Deutsche Soziologie der Gegenwart*. Secondly some of the problems posed by Weber now appear strangely familiar to present-day France. Mommsen was not wrong to point out the relationship between the constitution of the Fifth French Republic and Max Weber's ideas on constitutions. Finally—and this is the decisive reason—the European community has become a real experience for us to such a point that it behoves us all, sociologists and laymen, to think hard about nationalism (or yesterday's nationalisms) and about power-politics. Nevertheless, I would not forget Weber's distinction between science and politics, although the way in which he himself practiced this distinction was not always exemplary. It is a good thing not to confuse facts and values, reality and desires. Furthermore, one should take care to see the world as it is and not as one would wish it to be, or as one fears it may be: for a pessimistic distortion inspired by the desire to show that power-politics are inevitable and indispensable is no less to be feared than an idealistic distortion.

What exactly do we mean here by "power-politics"? It seems to me that two definitions can be put forward; one narrow, the other broad. Either one calls "power-politics" politics as practiced between states, politics subjected to competition between powers because it is not subject to any laws, any tribunal, any supranational authority. In this sense, all foreign politics, up to and including our own times, has always been power-politics, however diverse the conditions of the political units, and the relations between these units. Or else one can term "power-politics" any form of politics even within one state, which has power as its objective and/or its principal means. In this second sense, all power is at least partially power-politics. Politics seems to be all the more "power-politics" the more analysis emphasizes sovereignty (*Herrschaft*) and struggle (*Kampf*).

Whether we keep the first or second definition, Weber, as both a politician and sociologist, is a typical "power-politician." He belongs to the posterity of Machiavelli as much as to the contemporaries of Nietzsche. He would have rejected as meaningless the question: "Which is the best regime?" The struggle for power (*Macht* or *Herrschaft*) between classes and individuals seemed to him the essence, or if we prefer the constant theme of politics. A people or a person without the will to power was, according to him, outside the sphere of politics. Liberal and parliamentary institutions became under his pen necessary conditions for a nation's role in the world. He sometimes recommended them so that they should be proof that one people, the German people, was capable of playing the part of a great power.

Only master races have a vocation to climb the ladder of world development. If peoples who do not possess this profound quality try to do it, not only the sure instinct of other nations will oppose them, but they will also come internally to grief in the attempt. By "master-race" we do not understand that ugly "parvenu" mask made out of it by people whose feeling of national dignity allows them to be told what "Deutschtum" is by an English turncoat like Houston Stewart Chamberlain. But surely a nation which only produced good civil servants, estimable office-workers, honest shopkeepers, efficient scholars and technicians and faithful servants, and furthermore submitted to an uncontrolled hierarchy of officials using pseudo-monarchic phrases could never be a master-race, and would do better to go about its daily business, instead of having the vanity to concern itself about world destinies. Let us hear no more about "world politics" if the old conditions return. And writers who are addicted to conservative phrases will wait in vain for Germans to develop real dignity abroad, if at home they remain exclusively the sphere of activity of a mere bureaucracy— however purely technical or efficient—and are even pleased when learned clerics discuss whether the nation is "ripe" enough for this or that form of government. The will to impotence at home, which the scholars preach, has nothing to do with the "will to power" in the world, which has been so noisily proclaimed.[2]

I have quoted this passage because it contains all the main themes of Weber's concept of "power-politics." Theoretically all politics, home and foreign, is above all a struggle between nations, classes or individuals. Only those individuals animated by the will to power take part in this struggle, and are therefore fitted for politics. Weber never indicated explicitly any difference of character between the internal and external struggle. Like Machiavelli, he found struggle everywhere, but again like Machiavelli, he put external politics first, and set as his goal the unity of his nation (in this case the German nation) so that it could influence the course of universal history. A people of citizens and not of subjects, a people which has given itself liberal institutions, and takes part in the struggle for power instead of submitting passively to traditional or bureaucratic authority—only such a people can aspire as a "master-race" to take part in world politics, and this union of parliamentarianism and imperialist nationalism is certainly typical of Weber's thinking. However, Weber would not have granted it more than circumstantial value, or should not have done so. In the period of capitalism in Wilhelminian Germany, because the patriarchal authority of the emperor and the junkers was thenceforth anachronistic or ineffective, because civil servants by profession had no feeling for politics, i.e., for struggle, Max Weber demanded the democratization or parliamentarization of the regime. But I think Weber was too much of a historian and a pessimist to declare that master-

races are always free races. It is possible that a synthesis of liberalism and imperialism might have corresponded to Weber's scale of
values: to justify parliamentarianism by national interest, by the nation's power-interests, ought to lend an instrumental nature to spontaneous feelings of preference or perhaps even more to violent
antipathies.

If I keep to the second and broader meaning of power-politics, this
paper would to some extent deal with the whole of Weber's political
sociology. As such an undertaking is out of the question, I propose to
retain the first meaning of the concept of power-politics, i.e., external
politics, the rivalry of states which, being beyond the authority of
common law or a tribunal, are obliged to execute justice themselves,
and so to depend for themselves, their security, their existence, on
their own strength, and on their alliances: if we abide by this definition of power-politics, we must immediately make this first observation. Max Weber as sociologist wrote little about the struggle between
states, about nations and empires, about the relations between culture
and power. To be sure, the chapter in *Wirtschaft und Gesellschaft* which
would have been devoted to what one might call a sociology of international relations remained unfinished.[3] If he had had time, Weber
would probably have enriched this section by using his historical erudition. One unrivalled fact is nevertheless incontestable. Weber's nationalism was anterior to his sociological research, anterior to his
scientific work; he found it while living at the heart of Wilhelminian
Germany, while he was studying, and he absorbed it and made it his
own, unhesitatingly, and it seems, without profound reflection. On
many points Weber retained the teaching contained in Treitschke's
famous lectures on politics, though his philosophy is more pessimistic
and possibly more tragic.

He had decided once and for all that the supreme value to which
he would subordinate everything in politics, the god (or demon) to
which he had sworn loyalty, was the greatness of the German nation.
I use the term greatness (Grösse) although it is not Weber's own: he
more often speaks of *Macht* (power), *Machtinteressen* (power-interests),
Machtprestige (power-prestige), and *Weltpolitik* (international politics).
My reason for choosing the equivocal term "greatness" is that Weber
always suggests a link between power and culture. The German people are a people of culture (*Kulturvolk*). Power is certainly the aim,
but is also the condition for the dissemination of culture. Germany as
a great power is responsible to future generations for the kind of culture mankind will have.

It is not the Danes, Swiss, Dutch or Norwegians, whom future generations, our own descendants, will hold responsible if world power—that is, the power to shape the nature of culture in the future—is shared between the regulations of Russian officials on the one hand and the conventions of Anglo-Saxon society on the other, with perhaps a touch of Latin *raison*. It is we, the Germans. And rightly so.[4]

Weber admitted unhesitatingly the double solidarity of culture and nation: "All culture is national and remains so today, and all the more so, the more democratic become in extent and kind the external means of culture,"[5] and of the power of the nation and the diffusion of culture. To be sure, in the unfinished chapter of *Wirtschaft und Gesellschaft* he points out the interdependence of the extent or prestige of culture on the one hand, and military or political power on the other. He does not conclude from this that this power is favorable to the quality of the culture. Here is the passage as it figures in a footnote:

The prestige of culture and the prestige of power are clearly linked. Every victorious war promoted the prestige of culture (Germany, Japan, etc.)—whether it does the development of culture any good is another matter, incapable of value-free solution. Certainly not unequivocally (Germany after 1870) nor according to empirically palpable signs: pure art and literature of a German nature did not arise from the political centre of Germany.

Two observations on this passage: history which claimed to be "value-free" to the point of not passing any judgment on the quality of works would be strangely impoverished. It is striking that power, being the cause not of the quality, but of the diffusion or of the prestige (once again!) of culture, should be kept by Weber as the ultimate goal.

Weber's originality does not consist in adhering to this nationalism, which was fairly common at the end of the last century, nor in the passion with which he proclaimed the need for "world-politics" as an inevitable consequence and ultimate justification of Bismarck's work. Weber seems to me original and different from his contemporaries when he insists on the diabolical character of power and on the sacrifices demanded by the power-state. Treitschke, in his lectures on politics, found small states somewhat ridiculous. Weber is glad that a Germanism exists outside the Germany which has become a "national power-state" (*ein nationaler Machtstaat*).

> We too have every reason to thank Providence that there is a Germanism outside the national power-state. Not only simple, middle-class virtues, and genuine democracy, which has never yet been realised in a large power-state, but far more intimate and lasting values can only bloom on the territory of communities which renounce political power. Even those artistically inclined: such a true German as Gottfried Keller could never have become so original and individual in the midst of an army camp such as our state is inevitably becoming. (G.P.S., p. 60)

As far as the relations between nation and state, nationalism and imperialism are concerned, Weber belongs to his time, he shares its conceptions and its uncertainties. On the one hand he recognizes and underlines the strength of national claims, the aspiration of all self-conscious nationalities towards autonomy, even independence. On the other, he indignantly opposes the idea of compromise agreement about Lorraine. As for a plebiscite in Alsace, the very idea seems to him ridiculous.[6] Weber did not want non-German or hostile peoples to be absorbed in the Reich. But at the same time he was very far from subscribing unreservedly to the principle of nationalities, whatever form this might take. The splitting-up of Central Europe into states called national (but which would inevitably contain some national minorities) seemed to him neither desirable nor capable of realization.[7] He was led to conceive of a policy both national and imperial which would have reconciled the power-interests of the Reich with certain claims of other nationalities.

Having submitted that Russia was the chief enemy of the Reich, the only one who could question its very existence, he recommended during the First World War a German polity favorable to Poland, less out of sympathy with Polish claims than from concern for the German national interests.[8] Autonomous states protected militarily by the Reich, linked with it economically, would constitute the best protection against the threat of Grand Russian Imperialism. However—and this is indicative of the spirit of the times—Weber never went so far as to admit total independence of the Polish state, any more than he thought of sacrificing to the explicit desires of the people military guarantees or political advantages in the West. Characteristic of Weber on all these points is the almost total absence of ideological justification. It seems to me he was indifferent to the Franco-German dialogue about Alsace: should the German character of this imperialist province overrule the actual wishes of the people of Alsace? In the same way he abstained from any complex and subtle analysis of the "principle of nationalities." He recorded the variable strength of national feelings[9] and from this deduced quite realistically the danger of annexations in Europe and also the chances of mobilizing national feelings in Eastern Europe against the empire of the Tsars and for the Reich. He rarely advanced moral and idealist arguments in favor of any particular diplomacy—and when he did it was implicitly rather than explicitly. The final aim was arbitrary in the sense that no one—not even a German—was obliged to take as his supreme objective the power-interests of the Reich. As these power-interests were supposed to be inseparable from the interests of culture (at least of culture-prestige) they were surrounded by a sort of spiritual halo. Once the choice has been made, politics should consult reality at every moment in order to determine what is possible, with a view to reaching the ultimate goal, without caring too much about the morality or immorality of the measures it takes or recommends. If it does not care about them, it is not because of immorality but because of intellectual honesty. "For everything which shares in the possessions of the power-state is involved in the legality of the 'power-pragma' which dominates all political history."[10]

If this analysis is correct, Weber's national and imperial ideas must have been typical both of his times and his generation,[11] moderate in their objective and devoid of any phrase-making in their formulation. Germany was exposed particularly to peril from the East, the Tsarist empire of Grand-Russian imperialism: he hoped therefore until the final catastrophe of 1919 that the peace terms would be such as not to exclude the easing of relations with Great Britain and France. He probably had illusions as to what this easing would entail, but there again, if he was perhaps lacking in clearsightedness, he had more of it than most of his contemporaries.

It would be easy, but in my opinion without interest, to go into Weber's opinions in detail, to follow their variations from the famous Inaugural Speech to the pro-Polish writings during the war. These have often been studied and would distract us from fundamental problems.

Western political thinkers have always recorded as an obvious fact the heterogeneity of internal and external politics. When Hobbes, in his *Leviathan*, looks for an illustration of the state of nature and describes relations between the Sovereigns, he gives a radical expression to a classical idea. Weber, who defines the state as having the monopoly of legitimate violence, should logically recognize the heterogeneity between the violent rivalry of states and the rivalry, which is subject to law, between individuals and classes within a state. Now the fact is that Weber, who obviously admitted this heterogeneity, has rather blurred the distinction. It seems to me he was impressed and to some extent influenced by Darwin's vision of social reality. For example:

Whoever draws even a penny income which others have to pay—directly or indirectly—whoever possesses any commodities or used consumer goods produced by the sweat of another's brow and not his own, owes his life to the waging of that loveless, pitiless struggle for existence, which bourgeois phraseology terms "working peaceably for culture" (*Kulturarbeit*)—another form of the conflict between men, in which not millions, but hundred of millions decline and waste away in body and soul, year in, year out, or lead an existence to which any kind of recognizable "meaning" is really infinitely more alien than it is to responsibility which everyone has (and this includes women, for they too are waging "war," if they do their duty) for honour and that means simply—for the historical duties of the people, which depend on fate.[12]

This passage comes from his writing during the Great War. But more than twenty years previously, in his Inaugural Speech, similar ideas are expressed with the same force.

Even under the guise of "peace" the economic struggle between nationalities goes its way: the German peasants and labourers in the East are not being driven from the soil by politically superior enemies in open battle: in the silent barren struggle of everyday economic life they are on the losing side, even though faced by an actually inferior race, and leave their homes and proceed towards decline in an obscure future. There is no peace in the economic struggle for existence: only those who take the appearance of peace for the truth can believe that the future holds peace and enjoyment of life for our descendants. (G.P.S., pp. 17–18)

And again:

In place of the dream of peace and human happiness, there stands over the doorway to the unknown future of mankind's history: "abandon hope, all ye that enter here."

Not how the men of the future will feel, but what they will be like, is the question which occupies our thoughts about the time coming after our own generation, the question which actually is at the base of every economic task. It is not well-being we want to cultivate in men, but those qualities which we feel to constitute human greatness and the nobility of our nature.

And yet again:

It is not peace and human happiness that we have to hand on to our descendants, but the eternal struggle for the maintenance and cultivation of our national characteristics. And we must not yield to the optimistic hope that the work may be done in our case with the highest possible development of economic culture and that selection will then by itself help the more highly developed to victory in a free and "peaceful" economic struggle.

Our descendants will not hold us responsible before history primarily for the kind of economic organisation that we hand down to them, but for the measure of elbow-room which we win and bequeath to them. In the last resort processes of economic development, which are a nation's power-interests, are also struggles for power, when they are in question. These are the final and decisive interests of a nation to whose service its economic policy has to be harnessed. The science of economic policy is a political science. It is a servant of politics, not the day-to-day politics of those individuals and classes possessing power at any particular time but of the nation's permanent interests in power-politics. And the national state is for us not an indeterminate something, which one thinks should be all the more highly regarded, the more it is wrapped in mystical obscurity, but is the nation's temporal power-organisation, and in this national state the final criterion of economic consideration is the *raison d'état*. (p. 20)

I think these frequently quoted passages reveal what one must call Weber's *Weltanschauung*, with a Darwinian component (the struggle for life), a Nietzschean component (not the happiness of mankind, but the greatness of man), an economic component (the persistent scarcity of wealth—the ineradicable poverty of peoples), a Marxist component[13] (each class has its own interests, and the interests of any one class, even the dominant one, do not necessarily coincide with the lasting interests of the national community); and finally a national component, i.e. the interest of the nation as a whole, must outweigh all others, since nationalism is the result of a decision and not of deeds.

When I read Max Weber for the first time thirty years ago, I was particularly struck by the lesson of intellectual courage and modesty contained in his work. I still believe that his work contains a lesson which remains valid for us. But today I also realize that this thinking, which claims to be free of all illusion, stems from metaphysics, and a pessimistic vision of the world.

Power-politics between nations—of which wars are a normal expression and inevitable sanction—does not seem to Weber a survival from past ages or a negation of man's striving towards culture but one form among others all basically equally cruel, of the struggle for existence or of the struggle between classes and nations. In other words, a metaphysics, partly Darwinian, partly Nietzschean, of the struggle for life, tends to reduce the extent of the opposition between peace and war, between the people's economic rivalry and the states' struggle for power. Violence is not less violent for being camouflaged. If the same word *Macht* denotes the stakes of the struggle within a state, and the struggle between states, this is because the stakes are basically the same. In the one as in the other, it is a matter of knowing who is winning, who is in command, what share of available space or resources each class or each people will snatch for itself. This philosophy is no longer fashionable, for various reasons. Vulgarized and interpreted by barbarians, it has led to orgies of barbarism. Also, modern economics has proved false many judgments which specialists did not hesitate half a century ago to dignify by the name of scientific truth. Max Weber, like many of his contemporaries, but unlike the liberal economists, does not seem to doubt that the political power of a state commands the economic development of the nations. He speaks and writes as if the standard of living of the working classes depended ultimately on the arbitrament of war. In this respect, Weber does not belong to our times. We know today—and it would not have been impossible to know sixty years ago—that military strength is neither a necessary condition nor a sufficient condition for material prosperity.

Please understand me aright. Weber had chosen the power of the national state as the ultimate value, and this choice was free and arbitrary. Even if he had known that Wilhelminian Germany had no need of colonies either for the development of its culture or for the well-being of the working class, he would not necessarily have altered his decision: power-interests were a goal in themselves, and it remains true that the dissemination of culture has some connection with the power of the nation to which it is linked. But one's image of the world would no longer be the same if the struggle between classes and nations had as its main, if not exclusive, object control or power, and not well-being and life itself.

It is true that we are in danger today of committing the opposite error from Weber's. Within nations, as well as between them, social relationships contain an element of conflict which can be called respectively competition, contest, rivalry or struggle. The object of conflict is varied and sometimes the honor of winning is the sole reward. But from the moment when neither existence nor wealth constitutes the stakes, when the struggle is essentially political, that is to say it decides primarily who is to be in command, the distinction becomes more decisive between the modalities, the means, the rules of the various conflicts. A world without conflict is effectively inconceivable. A world in which classes and nations would no longer be engaged in a struggle for existence (*Kampf ums Dasein*) is not inconceivable. In any case, the difference between violent and non-violent forms of combat is regaining its full implication. The victor on the *Wahlschlacht-feld*, the electoral battlefield, differs in nature, not in degree, from the victor on the military battlefield.

The Darwinian–Nietzschean view of the world constitutes a framework within which Weber's conception of *Machtpolitik* is integrated. Polytheism, the plurality of incompatible values, constitutes the other basic idea in Weber's philosophy of power.

Weber, as we know, started from the Kantian or neo-Kantian opposition between what is and what should be, between facts and values. He did not reduce what should be to a moral system but he made morality itself one sphere of values among others. He added that the spheres of values are not only independent of each other, but are in irreconcilable conflict. A thing can be beautiful not *although* but *because* it is evil (*Les Fleurs du Mal*). From there he passes to two propositions both connected with *Machtpolitik*: the first, according to which there is no tribunal capable of deciding the relative values of German culture and French culture, the second according to which it is impossible to be at the same time a politician and a Christian (at least if Christian morality is that of the Sermon on the Mount), or again that each of us, in our actions, must choose between the morality of conviction and the morality of responsibility, and that the same action, according to the choice of one or the other set of ethics, will call forth a radically different appreciation.

These two propositions continued and are continuing to arouse impassioned polemics. The formula of polytheism is to some extent obvious. The artist is not as such a moral being, and a work of art is beautiful, not good. Each sphere of values contains a specific finality, a proper sense. The warrior's morality is not that of the saint or philosopher. Each obeys his own laws. Each nation expresses itself in a certain scheme of values, is proud of certain achievements. Who could be sufficiently detached and just to decide this point between these schemes of values and these achievements? Up to this point we all follow Max Weber. Beyond it there arise questions and objections. Let us look again at the famous passage in *Wissenschaft als Beruf* (*Science as a Vocation*), p. 545.

The impossibility of "scientific" representation of practical attitudes—except in the case of the discussion of ways and means for a purpose assumed to be definitive—follows from reasons which lie far deeper. It is in principle meaningless, because the various value-systems of the world are in insoluble conflict with each other. J. S. Mill, with whose philosophy I do not otherwise agree, said once, and correctly: if one starts out from pure experience, one arrives at polytheism. That is flatly expressed and sounds paradoxical, and yet there is some truth in it, which we still recognise today: that something can be holy not only *although* it is not beautiful, but *because* and *to the extent* that is not beautiful—we can find proof of this in Isaiah, chap. 53 and the 21st Psalm—and that something can be beautiful not only *although* but *to the extent* that it is not good we know since Nietzsche, and earlier still we find this embodied in Baudelaire's *Fleurs du Mal*, as he called his poems—and it is a commonplace to say that something can be true, although it is neither beautiful, nor holy nor good. But these are only the most elementary examples of this "war of the gods" between individual systems and values. How one will ever be able to decide "scientifically" between the respective values of French and German cultures, I do not know. Here different gods are in conflict and for all time. It is as it was in the ancient world, when men were not yet disenchanted about their gods and demons, but it is so in another sense: just as the Greeks sacrificed to Aphrodite and then to Apollo, and particularly to the gods of his own town, so it is still today, disenchanted, and divested of the mythical but inwardly sincere form of that behaviour. And over these gods and in their struggle fate rules, but certainly no "science."

It is true that no one can decide scientifically between French culture and German culture. But has the question any significance? Is it legitimate to pass from a fact—French and German cultures are different from each other—to the idea that gods are fighting each other till the end of time? I cannot help thinking that Weber, obsessed by the vision of struggle everywhere and at all times, came thereby to transform an incontestable but temporary rivalry of power into a war of the gods. There are circumstances in which power rivalries engage the very fate and soul of man. But such is not always the case.

Is it so obvious that "something can be beautiful not only *although* but *to the extent* that it is not good"? Is it consonant with the wisdom of nations that something can be true *although* and *to the extent* that it is neither beautiful nor holy nor good? The beauty of *Les Fleurs du Mal* has sometimes evil as its subject, but it does not originate in any intention of evil which might have inspired the poet: and if one can say that, thanks to the poet, vice assumes the appearance of beauty, it does not follow from this that vice is the cause or condition of beauty. Likewise, he who sees and says the truth, sees and says "that which is neither beautiful nor holy nor good." But the search for, or the expression of, truth is not therefore in conflict intrinsically, inevitably, inexplicably, with the search for beauty, holiness, or goodness.

But let us leave aside the wars of the gods which are only indirectly relevant to our subject, power-politics, and come to the opposition which dominates the whole of Weber's philosophy of action, the opposition of the two ethics of conviction and responsibility. No one is obliged, he tells us, to become involved in the sphere of politics, but if he does so, he must accept its inexorable laws. Since what is at stake in politics is power, and the division of power between classes and nations, he who claims to guide his companions, other members of his class or nation, must submit to the relentless exigencies of the struggle. It cannot be left out of account that this may require ways and means which, even if not evil, are at least dangerous. The ethics of responsibility are obviously not to be confused with *Machtpolitik*, and in an oft-quoted passage of *Politik als Beruf* he criticizes the cult of *Machtpolitik*.

> For although, or precisely because power is the inevitable means, and the striving for power one of the driving forces of all politics, there is no more harmful distortion of political strength than the "parvenu" boasting about power and the vain self-mirroring in a feeling of power, in short any worship of power itself. The mere "power-politician," as glorified by an enthusiastic cult, may make a strong impression, but this impression is in fact empty and meaningless. Here the critics of *Machtpolitik* are perfectly right. In the sudden inner collapse of typical protagonists of this attitude we have seen what inner weakness and impotence are concealed by this ostentatious but completely empty gesture. It is the product of a paltry superficial sophistication towards the meaning of human activity which is in no way related to the knowledge of the tragedy in all activity, particularly political activity, is really involved. (G.P.S., p. 437)

The ethical code of responsibility is defined not by the cult of power, nor by indifference to moral values, but by the acceptance of reality, by submission to the exigencies of action, and in extreme cases by the subordination of the salvation of one's soul to the salvation of the state. On the other hand, he who chooses the ethics of conviction obeys the commands of his faith, whatever the consequences.

In fact, Weber more or less confused two sets of antinomies: on the one hand that of *political action* with its necessary recourse to ways and means always dangerous, sometimes diabolical, and that of *Christian action* as suggested by the Sermon on the Mount or the teachings of Saint Francis (turn the other cheek, renounce the goods of this world): on the other hand, the antinomy of *thoughtful decision*, taking account of the possible consequences of the decision, and *immediate irrevocable choice* without any consideration of possible consequences.

These two antinomies do not entirely coincide. No politician can ever be a "real Christian" if the Sermon on the Mount contains the whole of Christian morality. No one has the right to ignore the consequences of his actions, and no one, in certain circumstances, can evade an inner exigency, whatever the risks of a decision dictated by a categorical imperative.

Weber, as a theoretician, claimed to follow the ethics of responsibility; as resolutely, and as practically and as soberly as possible he accepted *Machtpolitik*; that is to say, the use of ways and means required, within nations or between nations, by the struggle for power. He chose the ethics of responsibility and the obligations of power-politics from conviction, not out of personal interest, but out of devotion to the supreme value to which he had decided to adhere—the power of the Reich. For the politician who wants power for its own sake, or because of vanity or personal ambition, is a mere caricature of the true leader who only fulfils himself in the service of a cause greater than he.

In this political activity, Weber hardly behaved as a realist, and I am not sure whether, despite his knowledge and clearsightedness, he was really destined to become a leader of men. He more easily accepted in theory and in abstract than in fact the mediocre compromises, schemings and intrigues which are an integral part of effective politics as practiced under all regimes and particularly in democracies. Very often Weber appeared more sensitive, on his own and on others' behalf, to the value of a gesture, to the exemplary significance of a refusal than to the foreseeable consequences of his own decisions.

Weber was right to refuse illusions: politics are not carried on without conflict, non-violent conflict, and the ways and means of the conflict are not always compatible with the laws of Christ or simple morality. Two things however in this theory disturb me:

The first is the extreme and somewhat radical form given to the antinomy between the two moral codes, of responsibility and of conviction. Is it ever possible to ignore completely the consequences of a decision which one takes? Is it ever possible to disregard the moral judgment passed on a prevailing decision? I think Weber would have recognized this himself, but in declaring real an alternative which only becomes so in the most extreme circumstances, he runs a double risk: the risk of justifying on the one hand the false realists who scorn the moralist's reproach, on the other the false idealists who condemn indiscriminately all policies which do not correspond to the ideals, and who end by contributing consciously or otherwise to the destruction

of the existing order, to the advantage of blind revolutionaries or tyrants.

What is more, Weber is right to remind us that the eternal problem of justifying the means by the end has no theoretical solution.
But in affirming not only the heterogeneity of conflicts but their ir-
reconcilability, he prevents himself from founding his own authentic
system of values. Although he wrote that we could not live without a
minimum of human rights, he devalued his own values of liberalism
and parliamentarianism, by reducing them to mere ways and means in
the service of the Reich.

In the same way, I come to another objection: by setting the power-interests of the German nation as the ultimate goal, is not Weber
slipping towards some kind of nihilism? The nation's power, he says,
is favorable to the prestige, not the quality, of culture. If that be so,
can the power of the nation be an ultimate goal, the god to whom
one sacrifices everything? There is no question of denying the rivalry
between nations and one's duty to safeguard the nation's position on
the world's stage. But if the power of the nation, whatever its culture,
whoever governs it, whatever the means employed, is the supreme
value, what reason have we for saying "No" to what Weber would
have rejected with horror?

That, I think, is the main point we must think about. Weber affirmed and described the rivalry between European nations. If today
he seems to us to have over-estimated the importance of these conflicts and under-estimated the repercussions of a great war on the future of the European nations as a whole, he has at least, compared
with many of his contemporaries in Germany as well as in France,
the advantage of not having lost the sense of moderation and decen-
cy. He never lent his voice to the ravings of propaganda which were
rife on both sides. He did not question the national state as the supreme form of political community. (Perhaps this form has not been
ousted even today.) In any case, he belongs to his time in this respect
too. On the rights and duties of the great powers, on the diplomatic
rules of *Machtpolitik*, he expressed himself in the same way as his
contemporaries.

It remains to say that Weber, who as a sociologist is as up to date
today as yesterday, was not always, as a politician, in advance of his
times. Thus, he did not understand the implications of the Bolshevik
revolution nor foresee the totalitarian despotism of single-party rule.
Anxious to spare democracy the reign of politicians without vocation,
he emphasized the plebiscitary legitimacy of the charismatic leader,

unaware of the dangers which the following generation was to experience and suffer. He, who better than any other had understood the originality of modern civilization, did not understand the gap, at least potential in the technical age, between the power of arms and the prosperity of nations. As a bourgeois anti-Marxist, he invoked against Marx either the fate of bureaucracy or the efficacy of religious beliefs, but not the fact, common to all modern economies, of growth due to increased productivity.

True, it has not yet been proven that Weber's pessimistic Darwinian-Nietzschean view is the false one, and our view today the true one. The future lies open, and we do not know whether humanity will decide to destroy itself or to unite. But we do know that we can never again recognize in a nation's power-interests the final goal and a sacred value. Weber did, or believed he did, because the culture accumulated throughout the centuries seemed to him acquired forever and immune from the accidents of history. If he had known that in the name of power culture itself was in danger of being sacrificed, he would have realized that he was both too confident and too pessimistic—too confident when he put his trust in the elected leader and did not separate power from culture; too pessimistic when he could not imagine mankind at peace, or at least capable of submitting to rules the inevitable conflict between classes and nations. Weber after all betrayed himself in his theory of politics, for power was never his aim, neither for himself, nor for the nation. His thought and his life obeyed two values: truth and nobility. The man and the philosopher leave us an inheritance undiminished by the mistakes of the theoretician of *Machtpolitik*.

Notes

1. Wolfgang Mommsen, *Max Weber and Power Politics* (Chicago: University of Chicago Press, 1981). (Editor's note)

2. *Gesammelte politische Schriften*, 1st ed. (Munich: 1921), p. 259 (cited hereafter as G.P.S.).

3. *Wirtschaft und Gesellschaft*, 3rd ed. (1947) part 3, chap. III, pp. 619–30.

4. G.P.S., pp. 60–61.

5. Ibid., p. 47.

6. Letter to R. Michels, quoted by Wolfgang Mommsen, *Max Weber und die deutsche Politik, 1890–1920* (Tübingen: 1959), p. 258.

7. Perhaps he was right.

8. He had then abandoned his earlier ideas of a German colonization of the East, and his opposition to the immigration of Polish workers.

9. *Wirtschaft und Gesellschaft*, pp. 227–29.

10. G.P.S., p. 63.

11. I do not think Weber ever said clearly what he understood by international politics, nor what amount of colonial possessions would have satisfied the ambitions of the Reich.

12. G.P.S., p. 62.

13. In *Wirtschaft und Gesellschaft* there is yet another component: imperialism arising from capitalist interest (pp. 621 ff.). His exposition does not correspond to strict Marxism, since he thought a socialist economic system would be driven into imperialism even more violently. In another passage Weber explains the motives of imperialist expansion as not being exclusively economic.

Introduction

Aron and Machiavellianism

It is important to observe that Aron's prudence does not eliminate the antinomies of diplomatic–strategic conduct. Aron believes that the antinomy between law and struggle is a permanent antinomy characteristic of the "mixed" character of international society. A morality of prudence entails weighing and balancing partial logics and not following a complete or thoroughgoing logic to its potentially tragic conclusions. A 1943 essay by Aron entitled "French Thought in Exile: Jacques Maritain and the Quarrel over Machiavellianism" is helpful in differentiating Aron's "antinomic" prudence from a Thomistic prudence which emphasizes the radical limits of all Machiavellianisms and the priority of the "common good" as the standard guiding the conduct of statesmen. Maritain, in a series of writings dating from World War II, had attempted to trace a direct lineage from Machiavelli to the "Machiavellianisms" of the twentieth century, i.e., fascism and Nazism. The dialectical movement from the authentic thought of Machiavelli to the vulgar and destructive political "Machiavellianisms" is inevitable, according to Maritain, in that Machiavelli treated politics as an autonomous art, independent of all moral considerations. Politics became a technique independent of transpolitical guidance or considerations. But Maritain argued that "contrary to appearances, despite provisional successes" Machiavellianism "does not triumph in human history, in the last analysis, it is the art of causing misery to all mankind." For Maritain, Machiavellianism does not succeed because it brutally undermines the spirit, loyalties, and social cohesion that only a statesmanship reflecting and embodying the common good can sustain. Even the "moderate Machiavellianism" of traditional European statecraft associated with Elizabeth I, Mazarin, Frederick II, or Catherine the Great is bound to fail: it is a halfway house between real criminality and despotism and a residual respect for traditional European morality. Why not opt for a less subtle Machiavellianism,

49

for a brutal power-politics, if success is all that ultimately matters. Can a prince *appear* virtuous, humane, and religious as Machiavelli recommends in Chapter 18 of the *Prince* while embodying the audacious, inhuman, cruel, and self-preservative virtù that Machiavelli finally recommends to the Prince. The "aesthetic" project of Machiavelli, the autonomous art of political success, finally degenerates into tyranny, cruelty, and imperialism *tout court*. It dissolves social communities, depriving them of the moral strength and integrity which are more indicative of national strength than mere territorial aggrandizement. Maritain's argument is clear: justice may not preserve a state from ruin and destruction in the short term but in the long term "it tends by itself to this preservation."

Aron's response to Maritain is to reaffirm the antinomy between justice and success that Maritain tends to deny or at least strongly minimize. Not sharing Maritain's political science of natural law or his Christian faith, Aron nonetheless agrees that a rationalist philosophy is able to firmly mark the limits of that which belongs to Caesar as well as uphold the "imprescriptible rights of the person." Rationalism can recognize something higher than the art of politics. Aron calls that something "conscience." In addition, Aron rejects the nihilism of a power-politics which accepts the unlimited individual or state power as the single, supreme objective of political life. Such a power-politics leads to a dehumanization of men and societies and can, in vulgarized form, lead to limitless wars and struggle. But this "anti-Machiavellian philosophy," in itself true, does not dissolve the antinomies of international life. In domestic life, justice promotes the preservation of the state. It moderates partisanship and helps avoid the dangers of civil war. But Maritain's moralistic politics of the common good depends finally upon the primacy of domestic policy over foreign policy. Even principled, public-spirited statesmen in constitutionalist regimes who sincerely reject a vulgar Machiavellian philosophy are faced with situations where "the actual conditions of effective action (at least in the short run) and moral imperatives conflict." Aron accepts the practical primacy of foreign policy *in extreme situations* for all statesmen at all times. This is the partial truth contained in an otherwise dehumanizing "Machiavellian philosophy."[1] The vocation of the statesman is to see that his polity survives as a particular kind of community or regime. The difficulty is that extreme situations often are the norm in an international arena without an effective tribunal or an efficacious international law. One cannot settle here this immense difficulty for international relations and moral and political philosophy. This is not to suggest that the foreign policy of all states is, in the end, the same because all states which care about their survival resort to "Machiavellian" means to preserve themselves. To assess this is to abstract from the all-important dialectic of means and ends which is a central concern of political prudence and moderation. The character of regimes decisively affects the international behavior of states, and the citizens and statesmen of liberal polities are absolutely right to reject a philosophy of "power-politics." But, and this is the operative point, the dialectic of means and ends which is central to the problem of Machiavellianism knows no *theoretical* resolution. As long as this is the case, Machiavellianism, not as a philosophy but as the recognition of the *necessary* resort to force, fraud, and ruse in certain circumstances, will play a decisive role in the life of nations. But, and here Maritain is helpful, it is at best a partial logic, one aspect of social reality. Followed to its logic, it is destructive of the common good and the "interests" of a people. The morality of prudence is an effort on the part of Aron to make sure that the antinomy of law and struggle is not lived in a self-destructive manner, that is, tragically.

The following essay appears for the first time in English translation.

Notes

1. Aron is careful in his writings to differentiate the authentic thought of Machiavelli and the vulgarization of that thought which is "Machiavellianism." But he also recognizes that "Machiavellianism" is not completely foreign to the thought of the Florentine himself. It is fair to say that Aron wrote more about Machiavellianism than about Machiavelli himself perhaps because, as has been suggested, he was concerned above all about the theoretical and practical threats to human liberty and dignity in our century of totalitarianism and great wars. Aron began to write a study about the relationship between the thought of Machiavelli and the tyrannies of the twentieth century while in military service at a meteorological station during the "phoney war" between September 1939 and May 1940. Events interrupted Aron's ambitious project and the work was never completed. Three completed chapters, "The Machiavellianism of Machiavelli," "Pareto and the Machiavellianism of the Twentieth Century," and "The Comparison between Machiavelli and Pareto," as well as an unfinished chapter on "Machiavellianism and Tyrannies" have been published in a judiciously introduced and annotated volume, edited by Rémy Freymond, entitled *Machiavel et les tyrannies modernes* (Paris: Editions de Fallois, 1993). The book also includes later Aronian essays and reflections on Machiavelli and Machiavellianism as well as on modern totalitarianism. This work is indispensable for understanding the genesis and development, as well as the fundamental continuities, of Aron's thought. The uncompleted book on Machiavelli is the first full expression of the political

voice of the mature Aron. It is the bridge between his prewar philosophical work and his postwar turn to political, historical, and sociological reflection. The essay "French Thought in Exile: Jacques Maritain and the Quarrel over Machiavellianism" is a product of Aron's long meditation on the problem of Machiavellianism and provides a sense of the direction in which his earlier project was moving when it was precipitously interrupted by the exigencies of World War II.

French Thought in Exile: Jacques Maritain and the Quarrel over Machiavellianism

Raymond Aron

1943

For more than four centuries the quarrel over Machiavellianism has not ceased being of contemporary interest because at bottom this quarrel is eternal.[1] What goal ought he who undertakes to govern his fellow human beings propose to himself? What are the means which he has the right in conscience to use? This dual question will pose itself as long as the imperfection of men and the variety of their contradictory aspirations retain for force and injustice a both glaring and scandalous place in the destiny of collectivities.

Would Machiavelli himself have claimed or denied the paternity of what history has baptized as Machiavellianism? The learned have discussed this question for centuries. Common opinion, unencumbered by subtleties and knowing the *Prince* better than the *Discourses*, does not hesitate. To designate the politics of integral realism, common opinion has retained the name of him who both as a minister and a writer neither discovered nor created the practice but rather elaborated the theory.

Thus Jacques Maritain appears to us to be generally correct when, abstracting from erudite discussions, he imputes to Machiavelli responsibility at least for the phenomenon that philosophers call justification in conscience (*prise de conscience*). There always were and there will always be chiefs eager for riches and power, conquerors ready to act the part of the fox or the lion, as it serves their turn, to dispose of their rivals by assassination, to ground their domination in violence. However, as long as Christianity inspired the theoretically accepted teaching, the distinction between good and evil was maintained. Condottieri and Caesars already applied the lessons of the *Prince*, but at least they did not have the conviction that they acted well. Machiavelli is perhaps the first of the learned writers who contributed to give the wicked a clear conscience.

If the French in exile have discussed the problem of Machiavellianism, the monstrous excesses of totalitarian cynicism is not the sole reason. The realism of Maurras—of which Vichy diplomacy has often been seen as an application—was equally an incentive. In fact it was to Maurras in particular that Bernanos, who once belonged to the *Action français*, responded in *Scandal of the Truth* and *We Other French*, written before the disaster, and in the *Letter to the English*, written since 1940.

Bernanos' response is more that of a prophet than of a philosopher. He does not attack his adversaries, Maurras in particular, on the same level on which they place themselves. He shames them, he demonstrates, or rather he shows them the spiritual cowering and degradation to which the systematic obedience to calculations of force and opportunism, and indifference to the categorical imperatives of liberty and honor, "with which one does not reason," lead. Maritain, on the contrary, with less apparent fire, but with an ardent, secret passion, multiplies both arguments and reasons. He claims to establish the following theses:

1.   From Machiavelli's Machiavellianism to vulgar Machiavellianism, and then from the latter to total Machiavellianism, there is an irresistible movement.

2.   Politics, far from being an autonomous art, is subordinate to morality and has for its final objective the common good, rather than power.

3.   Contrary to appearances, and despite provisional successes, Machiavellianism does not triumph in human history; in the last analysis, it is the art of causing misery to all mankind.[2]

The evolution from Machiavelli to Hitler which Maritain briefly retraces already has become, so to speak, classic. It will be sufficient therefore to state its essential stages. Machiavelli observed the effective conduct of men and claimed to derive from his observations the rules of success. From experience—and also from a radical pessimism about human nature—he concluded the necessity of the means of force and fraud that religion and morality reprove but which prudence recommends. However, he did not deny the precepts whose violation he counselled. He limited himself to abstracting from them, laying down as a principle that the man of action ought to ask himself only about the modalities of success. In addition, he was very far from systematically praising brutality, lying or deception. Quite the contrary, in particular in the *Discourses*, he insisted upon the institutions and human qualities—meritorious in any view—which were the grandeur of the Roman Republic and whose return he wished for to a torn and impotent Italy. Finally, he envisaged politics like an artist; he saw in power and conquests works to create, comparable to sculptures, not acts to be accomplished by a person whose entire existence is ordered to a spiritual vocation. Virtue (*virtù*), a mixture of resolve, finesse and style, the supreme praise the Florentine reserved for those he placed the highest, is rather an aesthetic transposition of the Aristotelian conception of virtue.

Thus reduced to its logical structure (abstracting from the astrological and cosmological conceptions in which it is embedded), Machiavelli's Machiavellianism was undermined by a fundamental contradiction. "It presupposes, essentially, the radical uprooting of moral values in the mind of the political artist and, at the same time, it presupposes the existence and vital presence of moral values, or moral beliefs in other men, in the entire human material that the Prince is to manage and dominate." Montesquieu, too, had noted the impossibility, in the long run, of safeguarding the morality of a people whose leaders pride themselves on disdaining all divine and human laws. To be sure, Machiavelli responded that the statesman always ought to preserve the appearances of virtue even while he secretly accumulates lies and crimes. But he places too much confidence in hypocrisy's resourcefulness. In practice and in time, the Machiavellianism of the elites shows itself, even when it claims to disguise itself, and it spreads even when it wants to restrict itself to a small number. The most complete totalitarian regime, the Hitlerian, instituted rather than limited directed corruption. By a dialectical overturning, Machiavellianism undoes the convictions, the customs, the traditional structures from which it profits and upon which it grounds itself. In the final account, the immoralism of their chiefs demoralizes nations.

Machiavellianism destroys itself in yet another way. To believe Maritain, vulgar Machiavellianism, as it was practiced for centuries, as it was interpreted by Henry VIII and Elizabeth I, Mazarin and Richelieu, Frederick II and Catherine the Great, does not reject entirely the idea of the common good, nor does it reject the use of evil as an efficacious means. The combination of these elements however is fundamentally unstable. The idea of the common good had become so confused that it was more and more confounded with territorial aggrandizement and power. Moreover, if it is lawful to employ immoral means with a good conscience, why limit oneself to limited evil? If "violence without measure, injustice without limit, lies and immorality without limits" does better, why stop halfway?

All the barriers which still limit political realism's ravages disappear. One no longer only violates the rules of morality; they are denied, whether one declares them inapplicable to the political order, or whether one rules them out by unmasking them, by exposing them as the camouflage of the instincts. One no longer only moderately uses immoral means; they are used totally, either with the ferocious rationality of the technician, or with the annihilating desire of wicked men, anxious to pervert souls as much as to destroy bodies. The leader who employs the techniques of success is no longer an artist, concerned for beauty. Machiavellianism becomes so carried away by demonic impulses, by the unlimited desire for temporal grandeur, by idolatry before violence and the state. No longer simply political, it becomes "a religion, a prophetic, mystical enthusiasm."

Absolute or total Machiavellianism inevitably wins out over moderate Machiavellianism. In the game of deception and brutality, totalitarian regimes always will be stronger because they go to the very end of the lie, to the depths of bad faith, to the full exploitation of human lowness and weakness. In the end, however, this victory is a defeat for all; it becomes a means of extending human unhappiness. The only hope that remains is victory over Machiavellianism. And the principle of this victory must be a spiritual conversion which restores to politics its spiritual meaning, beyond Machiavelli's aestheticism and Hitler's biologism.

The end of Machiavellianism, whose necessity Maritain proclaims but which he refrains from stating, would be precisely this conversion. It would be defined above all by a double refusal: a refusal to consider politics as an art of success independent of morality, and a refusal to employ evil, even in order to succeed. In response to a politics which offers the kingdom of this world at the price of one's soul, the Christian says no. Conscious of "his destiny as a person, of his immortal soul, his final end and external life," man rejects the Machiavellian temptation, the temptation of the political order posing as absolute and presenting itself as the supreme goal, that is to say, he rejects the demonic temptation. "The State and politics, when they are really separated from ethics, are the kingdom of the demonic principalities of which St. Paul spoke, the pagan empire is the Empire of Man making itself God, the exact opposite of the Kingdom of the Incarnation and Redemption." Every Holy Empire whose Caesar, writes Maritain, be he a Christian, socialist dictator, or Dostoievsky's Grand Inquisitor, wants to establish the final kingdom of God or the final kingdom of man on earth has the same transcendent meaning which calls forth the same response from Christ: Get thee hence, Satan. The Christian must be ready to assume all the risks of the temporal adventure of politics, but not to engage his full person. "Man is wholly a part of the political community, but he is not a part in the sense of all of himself and all that is in him . . . his immortal soul and his God are not at the service of the State." However, this refusal—obvious to the Christian—does not resolve the quarrel of Machiavellianism. Because, if it is true, as is thought ordinarily, that the art of success normally entails the use of injustice, and if morality and justice lead to the ruin of cities, one must conclude that a Christian can hardly be a statesman or that the statesman can hardly act as a Christian. One can conceive that a nation, in a unique situation would prefer martyrdom to dishonor and death to shame, but the antinomy in the course of political life between success and morality would confirm Machiavellianism and assure its triumph. If the effective political means were lies, cruelty and violence, the protestations of intellectuals and writers would not hinder the reign of Machiavellianism.

That is why Maritain devotes his efforts to demonstrating the opposite position: *Machiavellianism does not succeed*. Of course, he does not deny that in certain cases and in the short run injustice pays! How many sovereigns owed their accession to the throne to the assassination of their rival or their brother? How many countries have attacked, conquered, exploited weaker neighbors? On the other hand, it clearly is not sufficient to be just in order to succeed. Neither glory nor military victories nor territorial increase are promised to virtuous nations. The political order belongs to the order of the routine: multiple causes determine events in the former. The destiny of a collectivity is the result of multiple phenomena, external and internal to the group. The moral quality of the individuals who compose it or of the institutions which shape it are but one of the determining factors.

All that one legitimately can ask for is that in history justice of itself tends to the good and injustice to evil. And Maritain does not hesitate to proclaim precisely this: "I maintain that justice, by its proper causality works towards well-being and success in the future, like sap, as long as it is healthy, works towards perfect fruit, and that Machiavellianism, by its proper causality, like a poison in the sap, towards the disease and death of the tree." His demonstration includes two kinds of arguments, one sort—ideological—relative to the definition of the political good, the other concerning the bonds between the moral quality of means and temporal success in the web of events.

Politics is a part of morality. It is distinguished from individual or personal morality and it includes an element of art and of technique because the reality to which it applies is composed simultaneously of matter and spirit. However, the essential truth of politics is and remains: politics, very far from being self-sufficient, is ordered to ethics, and is subordinated to the end proper to human existence. The end of politics in keeping with the true nature of things is the common good of a united people. And "this common good consists in a good life, that is, conformable to the essential exigencies and essential dignity of human nature, a life, at once morally correct and happy, of the social whole as such, of the assembled multitude, in such a way that the growing treasure and the heritage of sharable good things implied in this good life of the whole is shared and distributed in a certain manner to each individual part of the community."

The reference to the authentic good, even if it does not rule out the provisional success of force and injustice, if it does not eliminate the possibility of some definite defeats of morality, allows one at least to understand that justice as such tends to promote, and injustice as such to compromise, the common good. Why? Because justice reinforces and injustice dissolves the living unity, the profound convictions which make for the solidity of nations across the vicissitudes of military history. It is not enough when measuring the consequences of our acts and the ramifications of the means that are used to stop at immediate results. The success of a prince who conforms to the portrait drawn by Machiavelli, even if it lasts to the last day of his individual existence, is as yet only an *immediate success*. The true context in which it is proper to appreciate successes and defeats is the existence and duration of nations and political communities. Machiavellians measure the time of the maturation of political success by the short years of their personal activity. From this flows their impatience, sometimes their ephemeral triumphs but, in the long term, the ruin into which their proud works fall.

However, this just retribution in the long term is something of which no human insight can be guaranteed. First of all, even if the poisoned fruits of violence show themselves after the blow, the just person who has been its first victim knows *both* his sufferings and defeat and the provisional victory of his vanquisher, and not the ultimate disintegration of the nation which has followed the criminal leader. Moreover, admitting that justice in itself tends to cement the moral unity of a people and injustice to dissolve it, even admitting that by these traits themselves one tends to the success and the other to the defeat of the community, other factors of a material nature can cross this line of causality and cause even the worst communities, not the best, to survive.

"It happens sometimes that justice, even in the distant future, does not succeed in preserving a state from ruin and destruction. But justice tends by itself to that preservation." And one cannot argue against Providence. "God's justice is at work in time and history, it only reigns, however, in heaven and in hell. The concept of an infallible and complete retribution for human acts is a religious concept relating to the eternal destiny of human persons," and not the destiny of human communities in time and history.

It is true that the abortions of historical justice are less frequent than a superficial observation inclines one to admit. The human groupings who were destroyed by invasion most often had not attained the level of an authentic political community, or, like Greece at the time of the Roman conquest, had lost their soul. When a genuine and living community is engulfed by an invasion, such as Poland, it does not cease to live and to struggle against its oppression. Moreover, even if such a community ends by succumbing to the irresistible material weight of another power, beyond its death it continues to act on the rest of humanity, to transmit to it a part of its heritage, to cause the good that was in her to bear fruit. Even while the ravages of Machiavellianism, spilling over various frontiers, expands itself throughout the entire civilization which it is corrupting, the virtues of a martyred nation shed their splendor across humanity. The law of human extension, like that of political duration, illustrates the sterility, the noxiousness, the fundamental absurdity of Machiavellianism. "Like every other sort of egoism, divinized egoism is essentially blind."

On the basis of the same principle of the "self-destruction of Machiavellianism," every thinker—whether a believer or non-believer—who refuses to divinize the state and to posit as an absolute value the collective reality (of the state) easily will concur with Maritain.

1.   The political order is part of human reality and, as such, it cannot be detached from the whole of human reality without being removed from its true meaning. Even though the individual, in many diverse ways, depends upon the collectivity in which he lives and on the spiritual heritage he has received, whatever the obligations the community imposes upon the individual and that he must assume, a philosophy of rationalist inspiration which takes as its point of origin the conscience will mark as firmly as Maritain both the limits of what belongs to Caesar and the imprescriptible rights of the person.

2.   Politics cannot take as its unique or supreme objective power, without falling into a sort of nihilism. To desire at any price and on any term power, unlimited power, is both for the individual and the collectivity to fall into the idolatry of the state, it is to consent to dehumanization, it is, ultimately, to end up with the barbarism of to-

tal wars in which the infinite resources of science assist in the perfection of the ancient violence of wars of extermination.

However, once this anti-Machiavellian philosophy is accepted, the practical difficulties have only begun. If we were to suppose that, all at once, men were transformed, the problem would be solved. But if we still remain here on the earth, if we take men and nations as they are, it still remains to ask how ought, and how can the statesman act who sincerely desires to break with the practices of Machiavellianism? Maritain himself recognizes that in the real world justice ought to be armed with a sword, and that the prince ought to be prudent and cunning. It is however not easy to determine where legitimate cunning ends and immoral deceit begins. It is not easy to determine to what extent one can use force to maintain peace within nations and between them without engendering the evils inherent in the regimes founded on violence. To these questions it is impossible to give a general response. Antinomies and possible solutions are disclosed in the analysis of particular cases, in a sort of casuistry of political morality. Let us suppose, for example, peaceful nations, menaced by a devastating imperialism, seek an alliance with a great state. Let us suppose, moreover, that this latter lays down as conditions of its alliance demands which are in themselves excessive: ought one to abide by strict equity, at the risk of succumbing to an aggressor? When a "collaborator" offers to give the United Nations an undeniable service to bring territory and resources to them—what must be done? Ought one to sacrifice millions of lives on the pretext of not taking the dirty hand of another? When a preying people makes total, biological war against unarmed peoples, should one allow it the benefit of its crimes by sparing it the rigors it has inflicted upon others?

These examples have no other purpose than to illustrate a very simple idea: while one must oppose to Machiavellianism a radically different spirit, it is vain to imagine that one always has free choice of one's means. To be sure, the preceding examples are borrowed from a period of war, that is an epoch when, by definition, Machiavellianism reigns. But this very objection suggests a general proposition: the nature of the means that a politician, firmly hostile to Machiavellianism, will employ depends or will depend on the social milieu, the conditions in which the rivalry between individuals and states occurs, as much and more than on his intentions.

It is true, for example, that the struggle for power is more ferocious, more cynical, more immoral, as the state is on the verge of collapsing. During times of war and of revolution, when everything seems possible, when no tradition determines any longer the limits on

ambition, the battle between individuals and factions rages and feroc-
ity is given free course. Each one, seeing ahead of him unlimited
horizons, is ready to assume risks proportionate to the hoped-for success. The law of the jungle returns: whoever steps into the jungle thereby accepts, inevitably, some part in its procedures and perils.

This antinomy between the actual conditions of effective action (at
least in the short run) and moral imperatives appears not only in ex-
ceptional circumstances. It is linked to the imperfection of human nature, to the fundamental givens of political action. In truth political
action entails the recognition of the regularities observed in the conduct of individuals and crowds and utilizes foreseeable reactions to
attain predetermined goals. How can one mark the boundary between
the legitimate use of psychological and social mechanisms and the cynical exploitation of human weakness? One only has to think about the
case of propaganda to see the practical meaning and importance of
this question. Ideal politics would aim in its entirety at education. Cynical politics only aims at cultivating the good or bad traits which are
favorable to the prosperity of the state. Real politics oscillate between
these two extremes because neither leaders nor states can fail to concern themselves with the acquisition and maintenance of power. And
the techniques of power, neutral in themselves, imply the management
of men as they are. They more often manage to stir up hatreds than
love.

Maritain strongly affirms that the goal of politics is the common
good, not power, a formulation which ends in the primacy of internal
politics over foreign affairs, and which obliges one to prefer, in the
case of a necessary choice, justice in the relations among citizens and
classes to the glory and material greatness of the state. Even if one
accepts this formulation, power nonetheless remains an indispensable
condition of the common good. A nation which would disdain or, as
is said, would dishonor force would quickly discover that in the world
of men unarmed nations, like unarmed prophets, perish. Without doubt
the denial of Machiavellianism does not at all entail the rejection of
the just use of force. However, it nonetheless remains that the statesman must aim to increase the power of the community, at least as a
subordinate end, and that at each moment, he can be led to ask what
sacrifices he has the right to consent to in accordance with this secondary but real necessity. To imagine that these different goals—national unity founded on justice and well-being, and the material power
of the collectivity—call for, essentially and inevitably, the use of the
same methods would be to fall into a naive optimism.

Maritain attempts to mark the way of a politics simultaneously moral and realistic, somewhere between an abstract hypermoralism which, by proposing an unrealizable ideal, inclines men to cynicism and a Machiavellianism which resolutely occupies wickedness and evil. I fear, however, that he has not given sufficient recognition to the imperfection, the inertia, and the materiality of human and social nature. Or at least I fear that without denying it, he leaves in the shadows the part that art and technique play in politics. And conflicts arise when the techniques of the seizure, conservation, and organization of power require the use of force and fraud, and especially, more generally, an amoral management of men. Maritain moreover, it seems to me, simplifies somewhat the antinomies of existence while laying down the formulation "Machiavellianism does not succeed" and placing on the level of immediate successes all the victories of violence which spring up during the course of history and which so many times have engendered lasting works. Certainly, if the common good is posited as the purpose of politics and is defined by the ordered and equitable existence of a community, it is true, by definition so to speak, that injustice of itself tends to compromise, and justice to favor the common good. It is true that the quality of the means colors in a large way the ultimate results of action: in the long run the most solid faith poorly resists the denials and violence of Machiavellian tactics. All too often cynicism in the service of the ideal degenerates into cynicism pure and simple. But on the other side, it is no less true that there is from time to time a contradiction between the exigencies of temporal success and moral imperatives. Maritain is not unaware of this dialectical or, better yet, dramatic aspect of human existence insofar as it is political. For example, he announces that, without faith in Providence one cannot escape completely from the temptation of Machiavellianism. A purely natural morality would not suffice to furnish us the means to put its own laws into action. And is the situation of the Christian statesman very different? Will this latter resolve the contradictions between power and justice at the expense of the material prosperity of the community whose leadership he has assumed? Looking beyond the immediate consequences of his decision, will he trust God to assume the triumph of the good?

In any case, it is true that many statesmen, Christian and non-Christian, have decided this spiritual conflict differently, as though despite intentions and doctrines the political order ends by imposing the supremacy of the rule of efficacity. Were they wrong or right? We will not discuss this. It is sufficient to note one conclusion: what gives political life its somber grandeur is that statesmen come to do acts they detest because they believe themselves, in conscience and the depths of their soul, accountable for the common destiny.

Translated by Paul Seaton
with Daniel Mahoney

Notes

1. This essay appeared originally in *La France Libre*, vol. VI, no. 33, 1943, pp. 209–15, and in Nicolas Bavarez, *Raymond Aron, Qui suis-je?* (Lyons: Manufactures, 1986).

2. The problem of Machiavellianism appears in nearly all the political writings of Jacques Maritain. One can cite particularly "End of Machiavellianism" (*The Review of Politics*, January 1942) and "Politique et Religion" (*Lettres Française*, April 1942).

Part Two

Aron's Politic and Humane Liberalism

Introduction

Aron on Hayek and the Meaning of Liberalism

Everyone knows that Raymond Aron was a "liberal." But the word is characterized by so much ambiguity that it is important to clarify the distinctive nature of Aronian liberalism. Aron was a man of the left in the fundamental sense that in the dispute between the "Old Regime" and the "Revolution," that is to say, between premodern conservatism and modern egalitarianism, he stood unequivocally in the camp of equality and modernity. Aron's "values" are the preeminently "modern" values of liberty, equality, and universal citizenship. The equality of all citizens, universal enfranchisement, and the full variety of civic and religious freedoms are defended by Aron as the most precious acquisitions of modern peoples. But Aron shares with the right-wing of the triumphant modern or democratic party an opposition to the efforts by the extreme left to radicalize and universalize the demands of equality. A complete and consistent egalitarianism which makes no compromises with the inherited inequalities of previous eras and which ignores the reality and the claims of the capable, the intelligent, the industrious, and the ambitious is one which abstracts from the complexities and contradictions of social life and human nature. Aron always believed that social wholes necessarily contained an indestructible oligarchic dimension; it was demagogic and irresponsible to deny this fact in the name of "equality" and the maximization of "real freedom." Aron's liberal political sociology tries to educate modern democrats to the permanent but not necessarily tragic antinomies such as those between liberty, excellence, and equality which appear to be inherent in the very *structure* of collective existence. If Aron is widely characterized *today* as a man of the right, this stems in large part from his rejection of the illiberal left's efforts to overcome the antinomic character of modern democratic civilization.

Aron also was critical of the left's tendency to ignore the fundamental tenets of political economy. In their efforts to redistribute the wealth of nations, parties of the left often forgot about the irrevocable harm to productivity which could result from inattention to the incentives which motivate the entrepreneurial energies of economic man and the dangers to personal liberties which arise from an excessively regulatory, bureaucratic, and "tutelary" state. For all of these reasons, Aron, after a brief flirtation with socialism in the 1930s, remained a thoughtful and sympathetic partisan of the market and a growth economy. But Aron was no doctrinaire advocate of economic liberalism or principled opponent of a moderate and prudentially managed welfare state. There is no better illustration of the rich prudential and nondogmatic character of Aron's liberalism than his 1961 review essay of Friedrich A. Hayek's magisterial presentation of classical liberal political theory and political economy, *The Constitution of Liberty.*

Hayek attempted in that work to delineate the fundamental principles and themes of the constitution of liberty, of the regime or way of life, in the classical sense, of a free society. He emphasized two foundational principles of a liberal society, namely, the existence of a realm of nonconstraint or noncoercion in society, liberalism's private sector, and the recognition of the fact that only general or universal laws which apply to all citizens, to the governors and the governed alike, are capable of producing and maintaining the genuine rule of laws as opposed to the rule of men. Hayek's eloquent system joined a Lockean recognition of the primacy of private rights and a private sector as the core of liberty and liberalism, with a Rousseauian-Kantian emphasis on the dignity of law and the transcendence of *political rule* by the universalizability of laws which become the societal equivalent of natural laws. To these he added the essential insights of a classical liberal political economy.

Aron was not unsympathetic to the Hayekian construction and he admired both the principled and intransigent character of Hayek's presentation of the foundations of a "free, that is a good society." But he did have reservations about Hayek's system as a whole. These reservations can, I think, be summed up in one terse formulation: Hayek, like most liberals, succumbed to the temptation to do away with political rule and political prudence. He did not sufficiently understand that all societies, including the free society, necessarily entail an element of the rule of men over men. Liberty cannot be reduced to either the maintenance of a private sector of nonconstraint or the proclamation of universal, nondiscriminatory laws. A certain element of coercion is necessary in political life, especially in the areas of the economy and foreign affairs. Coercion and a certain degree of hierarchical subordination have hitherto played a part in all existing economic and political structures. There is no serious evidence that an industrial society can master social nature to the point where chiefs and subordinates will cease to be constituent elements of economic enterprises. Workers in modern enterprises are not, however, necessarily unfree. If coercion and hierarchy are perceived as being exercised in responsible ways, open to the rights, concerns, and well-being of workers, the lack of nonconstraint can be perceived by workers as being legitimate and equitable. Hayek abstracts from the important *psychological* dimension of liberty in a complex, hierarchical, but not necessarily oppressive society.

Similarly Hayek forgets an insight that is central to the political thought of the equally liberal John Locke. Because natural right is ineffective in the area of foreign affairs, because there is no tribunal to judge the actions of various states and the states must therefore help themselves, foreign affairs remains effectively intractable to the rule or government of law. Locke recognized the necessity of a federative power, practically exercised by the executive, which would prudently guide the commonwealth in the areas of war and peace. This federative power is limited but not finally controlled by the laws promulgated by the legislature. The executive–federative power must exercise *prerogative*—that is, authority which is beyond law. By abstracting from foreign affairs and the problem and necessity of the federative power's prerogative, Hayek is able to separate liberalism, defined as nonconstraint and the maintenance of general laws, from the problem of political liberty. But if chiefs are present not only in the economy but also in the polity, and if the political-military chief, the exerciser of the federative power, ultimately has primacy over the decision to make war and risk the lives of free citizens, political liberty and political participation appear to be like constituent elements of the constitution of liberty. If rule necessarily persists even in the constitution of liberty, citizens must have confidence in the intelligence and equity of those who play such a central role in shaping their destinies.

Aron also criticized the notion that the universality or generality of law can effectively substitute for a moral-political judgment of the justice and fairness of legislation. Laws can have the appearance of universality and yet be aimed discriminately at a particular majority or minority of society. There is no formula which can replace wisdom as an ingredient in the successful operation of a free society. Rule of law is at best an ideal but it loses its undoubted dignity when it takes on a formulaic character, when it is presented as a replacement for politics and prudence.

Hayek's liberalism is open to two more charges of depoliticizing the constitution of liberty. Like most liberals Hayek downplays the moral underpinnings of a free society. He knows that liberty must be exercised responsibly but he does not discuss in any adequate manner one of the great themes of the politic liberalism of Alexis de Tocqueville and Montesquieu, namely, the importance of sound mores for the maintenance, sustenance, and flourishing of a healthy, envigorated free society. He writes as if the moral foundations of a free society will take care of themselves. He does not discuss the issue of liberal civic education. Hayek is not a relativist but his relative abstraction from the problem of civic education leads him inexorably to the position that a free society can expect its citizens to choose their own gods or values without serious consequences for the integrity of the social order. He takes for granted that premodern capital which modern liberal civilization has inherited but has not always sufficiently appreciated. He assumes that men will act responsibly. Aron's recognition of the centrality of the problems of moral and civic education and his recognition of the fragility of all civilized order led him to recover the spirit of Tocqueville's position on the centrality of mores even, or especially, in the liberal order.

The last Aronian reservation is one we have already alluded to. Hayek is doctrinaire in his hostility to the welfare state. Hayek believes that the welfare state threatens liberty, weakens productivity, and threatens to plunge modern people down the road to serfdom, toward a tutelary or even worse form of despotism. Aron agrees in part: there can be an excessive form of redistributive and regulatory socialism which threatens the productive engines of a commercial society and which diminishes the liberties of citizens by pursuing the impossible dream of a radically egalitarian social order. Aron agreed that there could be a socialist road to penury and serfdom. But a social welfare liberalism or a moderate social democracy was also possible. Regardless, the welfare state in one form or another, despite its genuine difficulties, is an inevitable feature of our modern societies flowing from the very logic and nature of the representative commercial regime.

The Liberal Definition of Liberty reveals the "mixed" character of Aron's political reflection. He combines the two seemingly contradictory spirits of liberalism and politics. He is too much aware of the contradictory or antinomic character of social life to believe that liberalism can replace the government of men with the rule of law and administration, that is, put an end to history. Aron's is the rarest of liberalisms—a politic and political liberalism. He resists the temptation of liberals, as well as Marxists, to do away with politics.

Aron's review essay of Hayek's book appears here for the first time in English translation.

The Liberal Definition of Liberty: Concerning F. A. Hayek's *The Constitution of Liberty*

Raymond Aron

1961

F. A. Hayek's book was ignored—or all but ignored—in France, and many who ought to have read it in Great Britain and the United States have neglected it, because they were prejudiced against the theses of the author of the *Road to Serfdom*. Personally, I subscribe to the judgment of Professor J. W. N. Watkins:

> In any circumstances *The Constitution of Liberty* would have been an important book. Given the condition of political philosophy in the English-speaking world today, it is outstandingly important. In recent years contributions to political philosophy have consisted almost exclusively either of historical work, often of a high scholarly excellence but hardly attempting to bring the ideas discussed to bear on modern issues, or of occasional ballons d'essai which have not risen very high despite the absence of mooring lines.[1]

Whether one follows Hayek or not, whether one follows him all or part of the way, it is still a delight for the mind to read a systematic book in which a vigorous mind has attempted to develop a series of theses according to a rigorous logic, to stipulate, beginning from a few definitions, what a free society, that is, a good society, ought to be.

Therefore, the criticisms I will formulate must not create a false impression: they do not stop me from subscribing to the judgment I just reported and from admiring the breadth of the construction.

I

Let us examine closely the English title of the book: *The Constitution of Liberty*. The term "constitution" obviously has a richer meaning than its strictly juridical use. "Constitution" is taken in a sense in which it signifies with respect to society the equivalent of constitution, narrowly understood, vis-à-vis the political system. It determines the laws according to which common life is organized. On what conditions does this organization of society merit to be called liberal, that is, does it respect the liberty of individuals?

The inquiry has for its point of departure and its foundation a definition of *liberty*. Liberty is first of all defined negatively by the absence of coercion or constraint. But constraint is a concept not much more clear than liberty; it, in turn, calls for a definition (which the reader finds at the beginning of the second part). The initial definition—liberty (which in English is indifferently freedom and liberty) is nothing but the absence of constraint—nonetheless excludes three other ideas frequently linked in our time to the concept of liberty: participation in the political order or, more precisely, the choice of rulers by electoral process; the independence of a population governed by men of its own race or nationality, which rejects foreign masters; and, finally, the power of the individual or the collectivity to satisfy its desires or to attain its own ends. Nor should "internal liberty," the ability to choose intelligently or reasonably, be linked to the liberty Hayek wants to preserve or promote.

Thus defined, liberty becomes a negative but indivisible reality. Contrary to the counterrevolutionaries or conservatives who speak of liberties rather than of liberty, Hayek prefers the singular. Men are more or less free, that is, they are subject to more or less constraint, but their liberty does not divide into different rights or into separable powers. If they escape from constraint, they are free; or better, reduction of constraint gives the measure of their liberty.

This argument obviously supposes that the latter is itself an indivisible reality, although susceptible to more and less. This is the result of the following definition: "Coercion occurs when one man's actions are made to serve another man's will, not for his own but for the other's purpose."[2] And a little further: "Coercion implies both the threat of inflicting harm and the intention thereby to bring about certain conduct."[3] The essence of constraint is thus the threat of inflicting a sanction on another if he does not submit to our will, most often but not always by the use of force. He who suffers constraint loses the capacity to use his intelligence to choose his ends and his means. He becomes the instrument of the one whose will he obeys.

Since coercion is the control of the essential data of an individual's action by another, it can be prevented only by enabling the individual to secure for himself some private sphere where it is protected against such interference.[4]

The definition of constraint confirms the negative conception of liberty. The latter consists essentially in the sphere of decision and action reserved for each. He is free who is not a slave. He is free who has the legal status of a protected member of the community, he who does not run the risk of arbitrary arrest, who has the right to choose his work and to move about at his good pleasure.[5] Hayek evokes four rights, not four liberties, as an enumeration (neither exhaustive nor final) of what is normally contained in the private sphere reserved for each.

The fundamental questions raised by this philosophy of liberty derive from these initial definitions: (1) Is it possible to circumscribe from the outside the domain of constraint, to distinguish rigorously the different influences—constraining and non-constraining—that men have on one another? (2) In this attempt to distinguish, is it possible to maintain a radical separation between liberty—the sphere of private decision—and the other senses of liberty? (3) Is it legitimate to determine the good society or free society with reference to the sole criterion of liberty as non-constraint? We will attempt to respond to these three questions in the following pages.

Life in society implies the coordination of individual activities. In turn, this coordination requires rules, that is, the distinction between what is authorized and what is forbidden. It also requires a hierarchy of authority in no-matter-what collective enterprise, economic or military. Whether the objective is to kill a deer, to take an enemy's position, or to build a bridge, the acts of each—hunter, soldier, or worker—are and must be parts of a whole which only exists, entirely, in the mind of one or a few heads. Hunters, soldiers, and workers inevitably become the instruments of their leaders, subject to constraint—unless one uses another definition of constraint.

Hayek would probably admit that a soldier is not free. But this proposition—in one sense incontestable—is nonetheless troublesome, because the citizen who, by his vote, accepts obligatory military service, in a manner of speaking subscribes to the temporary alienation of his liberty. Constrained in his daily action, he morally consents to this constraint by his decision as a citizen. By defining liberty exclusively by the "sphere of individual decision," one loses the possibility of distinguishing between the situation of the individual who is forceably enrolled in a conquering army and that of the citizen who fulfills military obligations of which he, by his vote, was the author. Or, at least according to Hayek's notions, this distinction would have nothing to do with liberty.

Hayek responds almost directly to this objection:

> It would be difficult to maintain that a man who voluntarily but irrevocably has sold his services for a long period of years to a military organization such as the Foreign Legion remained free thereafter in our sense; or that a Jesuit who lives up to the ideals of the founder of his order and regards himself "as a corpse which has neither intelligence nor will" could be so described.[6]

Doubtlessly, the legionnaire and the Jesuit agree to obey the direct, specific will of another. But what operative value, what usefulness does the concept of non-liberty have according to Hayek's definition? Suppose a legionnaire who loves military life, who believes in the causes for which he fights and who has confidence in his officers: he will not experience any feeling of oppression.[7] Similarly, the Jesuit alienates his liberty in the sense that he renounces all or part of his private sphere of decision. Not free in Hayek's sense, he is constrained and permanently so. In this sense, he is oppressed, because "oppression which is perhaps as much a true opposite of liberty as coercion, should refer only to a state of continuous acts of coercion."[8]

It seems to me that the difficulty is owing to a too-large definition of constraint, apparent, moreover, in the text. Either there is constraint whenever there is alienation of the right of decision and personal initiative, and, in this case, all enterprises of the military type *involve* constraint; or constraint begins only when an individual becomes another's instrument *against his will* and cedes to him for fear of sanctions; in this case it is appropriate to introduce an area of *neutral* activity between liberty as personal activity and constraint effected by threat. An individual could hardly be called free, since he does not choose his object, his project or even his means, but he could hardly be said to be constrained or oppressed, since he acknowledges the necessity or (and) the legitimacy of the orders he obeys.

If, in the case of the legionnaire or the Jesuit, Hayek can claim that strictly speaking both choose servitude, he cannot make the same argument about the worker. By obeying the orders of the *foreman*, the engineer or the director, he obviously serves the purposes of another, he chooses neither his goals nor his procedures, he is threatened by sanctions in case of disobedience. Hayek probably is aware of this possible objection, since he makes use of the opposition—which is all-important in his eyes—between a *general law* and a *specific com-*

mand in order to reintroduce into the enterprise or domestic foyer a
sphere of individual liberty:

> The manner in which the aims and the knowledge that guide a particular
> action are distributed between the authority and performer is thus the
> most important distinction between general laws and specific command.
> . . . Such general instructions will already constitute rules of a kind,
> and the action under them will be guided by that of the acting persons.
> It will be the chief who decides what results are to be achieved, at
> what time, by whom, and perhaps by which means, but the particular
> manner in which they are brought about will be decided by the
> individuals responsible. The servants of a big household or the employers
> of a plant will thus be mostly occupied with the routine of carrying out
> standing orders, adopting them all the time to particular circumstances
> and only occasionally receiving specific commands.[9]

The preceding quote calls for two remarks: is it true that work, at
home or in business, consists essentially in executing permanent directives? Is it true that the worker's liberty is, or should be, measured
by the relation between these permanent directives and precise commands? Does liberty increase with the increase in the percentage of
the former and the decrease of the latter? I have doubts about both
propositions. The first proposition seems to me true for enterprises of
a certain type, but not for all. As for the second, it can only be posed
as a matter of semantics: by definition, the worker's liberty within an
enterprise will be measured by the amount of initiative he enjoys in
the carrying out of the permanent directives. However, the worker's
sentiment of liberty or oppression depends quite obviously on many
factors, with the extension of permanent directives and initiative in
execution being but one of these factors.

Let us bring these first analyses to a close: Hayek wanted to define liberty by the absence of constraint and constraint by an objectively identifiable situation. Since he declares every individual who
appears as an instrument at another's service as constrained, every
project conceived by one man and executed by many entails the constraint of those who do not command. Unless one interjects the notion of "threat" on the part of the chief and refusal or resistance on
that of those who execute. But on this hypothesis the accent changes:
it matters little that the individual does not choose his goals or his
means, what's essential is that the individual obeys a discipline he does
not approve, that he judges contrary to his rights or to fairness. But if
this subjective element is introduced into the definition of constraint,
one must introduce it also into the definition of liberty. No more than

obedience to specific commands entails constraint does submission to permanent directives or general laws guarantee liberty.

Of course, and this goes without saying, Hayek does not deny that life in society requires a certain amount of constraint. He does not deny that each one of us, in private life or interpersonal relations, is exposed to the risk of being constrained by neighbors, friends, even strangers. Nor does he deny that besides laws or public authority, customs and collective prejudices can constrain the individual. But he considers these latter risks of constraint to be weak compared to those created by the progressive retrenchment of the rule of law by the government or domination of men. It is not true, he says, that in a free society men rule over men: laws rule equally over governors and governed.

> The conception of freedom under law that is the chief concern of this book rests on the contention that when we obey laws, in the sense of general abstract rules laid down irrespective of their application to us, we are not subject to another man's will and are therefore free.[10]

And a little further:

> The fact is that, if "to rule" means to make men obey another's will, government has no such power to rule in a free society.[11]

Hayek links himself to a long and glorious tradition, which equates liberty with obedience to laws and which attempts to reduce as much as possible the control that some men exercise over others.

Hayek himself notes a first difficulty: a general, abstract law, applicable to all, nonetheless can restrict liberty. He admits that religion often has furnished the pretext for the establishment of rules felt to be extremely oppressive; he even admits that religious beliefs have been the sole reason why "general laws seriously restrictive of liberty have ever been universally enforced."[12]

The problem with this is dual: does obedience to general laws, as such, equal liberty as defined? Or, does the generality of law create a probability that they will not be oppressive? Hayek's thought on this point seems to me to fluctuate. He says laws can restrict liberty; he does not say that they can be "constraining" (submitting someone to the will of another man). He says that general laws can be felt to be "oppressive"; he does not say they are. They can't be oppressive, properly speaking, except when these general laws appear as the expression of the will of someone or a group of men. But if Hayek admits that a general law can express (while camouflaging) someone's will, the opposition upon which he founds his doctrine loses its rigidity.

Nothing is easier than to imagine laws conforming to the essence of legality and yet which can be felt to be "oppressive." If a law forbids all citizens from traveling abroad, it is not liberal, while being non-discriminatory. A law which is in fact discriminatory can be cast completely in general and abstract terms: for example, if, henceforth, no one has the right to own more than a third of the capital of a daily paper, only a small number of persons will be affected, but the form does not allow one to see if it is a "command" or a "law."

The generality of the law therefore does not allow one to affirm that its interdiction is not considered oppressive by those who are subject to it. Nor does it suffice to guarantee the elimination of the element of "personal command" which Hayek sees as the essence of constraint. Let us take sumptuary laws; they can be formulated in general rules: no one will have the right to possess more than so many hectares . . . no one will be able to spend more than so many millions . . . no one will have the right to manufacture such-and-such jewelry. . . . These envisage no one in particular but they aim at all who might fall within these categories. Now these laws, no matter how general, and although in principle they take in all persons, effectively concern only those who are in the situation of being able to do what is forbidden. What, then, distinguishes discriminatory laws from others?

Hayek suggests two answers: if a law applies equally to governors and governed, it is not discriminatory. Secondly, a law ought to be as acceptable to those it strikes as to those it does not concern. The first answer has a certain pragmatic value. One is tempted to admit, first, that, if the governors are subject to the same laws as the governed, "little that anybody may reasonably wish to do is likely to be prohibited."[13] However, a first exception (one recognized by Hayek) concerns "true believers" (whatever their religion), who do not hesitate to impose on others whatever they judge in accord with their faith. Let this faith be economic, let it proclaim, after Proudhon, that commerce and theft are equivalent, and the prohibition of private property in the instruments of production will become law. This law will exhibit all the formal characteristics of law. If, in his system, Hayek can condemn it, it is because the suppression of private property entails the reduction or elimination of the private sphere and the expansion of personal commands. It is easier to condemn certain laws by referring to the ideal of a sphere of personal action than by pointing to the generality of the law as proof that it is not oppressive.

As for the second criterion—that the laws which only apply to a category of persons ought to be acceptable to the members of this category as well as to the rest of the society—it ends up giving every minority group a moral right to veto legislation. Although this idea is not stated in a categoric manner, it comes up in attenuated form several times. Writing about the social services the state ought to finance by using constraint, Hayek says:

> It is not to be expected that there will ever be complete unanimity on the desirability of the extent of such services, and it is at last not obvious that coercing people to contribute to the achievement of ends in which they are not interested can be morally justified.[14]

The same argument is presented in connection with progressive taxes:

> What is required here is a rule which, while still leaving open the possibility of a majority's taxing itself to assist a minority, does not sanction a majority's imposing upon a minority whatever burden it regards as right.[15]

The law which provides for the progressivity of income tax is formally a law; general and abstract, it does not directly envisage particular individuals. Nonetheless, it represents a form of constraint because it channels individuals' revenues to ends determined by the state, i.e., other persons. However, given that some constraint by the state is inevitable, the question is to determine the limits within which state coercion is exercised legitimately. The non-discriminatory character of the coercion, or, in case of discrimination, the minority's acceptance of it, gives an external sign—as well as confirmation—of the fairness of the discrimination:

> If the classification of persons which the law must employ are to result neither in privilege nor in discrimination, they must rest on distinctions which those inside the group singled out, as well as those outside it, will recognize as relevant.[16]

Whatever one thinks of progressive taxes, it would be unreasonable to expect the rich minority to accept it as willingly as the poor majority. Either the former will complain of discrimination, or the latter will take umbrage at privileges. It is not the minority or the majority which will find the solution which will avoid discrimination and privilege, but rather the reasonable men of both groups. This is tantamount to saying that there is no objective criterion of non-discrimination and non-privilege (no more than there is an objective, external definition of constraint).

Based on this, I would be inclined to *call into* question an analogy which holds a position of primary importance in Hayek's philosophy: the general laws promulgated by the state can be compared to natural laws; they determine the conditions to which each of us ought to adapt or must master in order to act; they leave intact our personal sphere, our freedom of action. On the other hand, commands, whether they come from other persons or from the state, imply constraint.

Is it true that general rules can be considered as equivalent to natural laws? I do not think so. First of all, these days, men think otherwise. They know that laws, no matter how general, are the product of men; the fact that the law which requires two and a half years of military service allows no exceptions does not, in the eyes of those subject to it, render it like natural laws. In other words, this comparison does not agree with men's sentiments. And how could it be otherwise? Laws can be skirted; an ingenious individual can violate them with impunity; an honorable man can attempt to modify them. In any case, the generality of a legal interdiction or authorization does not have the same sense as physical possibility or impossibility. As Durkheim would have said, the connection between the violation of the law and its sanction is synthetic, that between an act and its consequences is analytic. Each one of us will deny, and rightly so, the assimilation of a social law to a natural law every time it appears to be unjust or absurd.

Hayek quite rightly refuses to circumscribe the sphere of personal autonomy, except for special circumstances of time and place. It was legitimate, he writes, for the state to impose religious conformity as long as men believed in collective responsibility towards some divinity. In order to define the borders of the protected zone, the important question is to know "whether the actions of other people that we wish to see prevented would actually interfere with the reasonable expectations of the protected person."[17] Otherwise put, the state is right to forbid what the individual of each epoch reasonably considers as not belonging to his personal sphere. This sphere is greater or smaller depending upon the society; the content of individual liberties varies historically. But, if this is true, how does the eternal definition of non-constraint, thanks to the generality of law, combine with the historicity of the delimitation of the individual sphere? To my mind, their reconciliation requires that the emphasis be placed less on the non-constraint of a general law than on the concrete character of the interdictions imposed by the law. Or else nothing would prohibit oppressive interdictions—in the form of general laws—which would render illegal the exercise of individual judgment in domains where the governed expect to enjoy it.

Once the historical, variable character of the limits of the individual sphere is posed, the other criteria—non-discrimination, generality of the rule, the reduction of the domain of specific commands—retain their significance. No one of them by itself is decisive, but together they suggest an ideal: a society or state which would leave to individual initiative a margin of operation as large as possible, where the governors would submit to the same obligations, to the same prohibitions and the same authorizations as simple citizens, where privileges and discrimination would be reduced to a minimum. But there is no objective, eternally valid definition of discrimination, just as there is no such definition of constraint and, consequently, of liberty.

Hayek's doctrine appears to me perfectly clear at the level it ordinarily placed itself, i.e., as a doctrine of what modern society ought to be. On the other hand, the philosophical foundations he wanted to give to this social ideal seem fragile to me. He wanted to define liberty by the absence of constraint and constraint by an objectively recognizable situation. But he failed to recognize the fact that all collective enterprises make of certain individuals the instruments of their chiefs, without, however, soldiers or workers considering themselves "oppressed." He laid down a radical difference between obedience to persons and submission to rules and ignored or neglected the fact that general rules also can be oppressive and that, in the last analysis, it is the relation between, on one hand, the content of interdictions and obligations and, on the other, the legitimate expectations of individuals which determines the actual measure of liberty in a given society.

Now we have to ask if, and to what extent, the critique of the philosophical foundations entails consequences concerning the socio-economic teaching itself.

II

The goal of a free society ought to be to limit as much as possible the government of men by men and to increase the government of men by laws. Such is, there is no doubt, the first imperative of liberalism as conceived by F. A. Hayek. It happens that I, too, share this ideal. The reservations I will register, therefore, will not have at their origin a different scale of values, but rather the consideration of some facts.

There has never been, nor is there today, one "human collectivity." There are "human communities." Each one finds itself, alternatively, in friendly and hostile, peaceful and belligerent relations with others. The conduct of foreign affairs belongs and can only belong to one or a few men. The designation of this man or these men takes place differently, depending upon the time and the regime. But the direction of foreign relations remains the task of men and not of laws. In his *Second Treatise*, Locke explicitly distinguishes two aspects or two modalities of executive power: on one hand, this power has the function of assuring the execution of the laws; on the other, that of treaties, of peace and war. Like most liberals, Hayek does not treat foreign affairs. He limits himself to indicating, in passing, that, provisionally, the world state appears to him a danger to individual liberty; in these conditions it is better to accommodate oneself to the plurality of states and to eventual wars.[18]

However, the federative power, to use Locke's term, continues the government of men by men and not by laws. In the matter of treaties, peace and war, writes Locke, there are hardly any laws or rules. In their mutual relations, states are subject to the obligations of natural right, but since there is neither tribunal nor police, they have no other recourse than to execute justice themselves. And men, not laws, decide as to what this "justice" requires. I fear that according to Hayek's definitions, all diplomatic action, or at least all action leading to war must be considered as "constraint" of the governed by the governors, the whole collectivity being the instrument of projects conceived by the governors alone. Wouldn't one say that this is not the case if the people have an intimate resonance with the decisions taken by its chiefs? The objection will not stand up within the frameworks of Hayek's thought, since constraint has been defined by the absence of personal choice, by the manipulation of individual circumstances or by threats in case of disobedience; all these traits are present each time diplomatic action obliges citizens to honor engagements made by their governors.

But if war and peace result from the action of men in power, how can one claim that the rule of laws leaves no room for the domination of men by men? One also thereby understands—without departing from Hayek's own intellectual system—why one cannot remain content with the definition of liberty as absence of constraint, with that absence guaranteed by the generality of law. Since there is no collectivity without foreign affairs, without the federative power, and since the latter is always exercised by men, citizens cannot not obey specific commands and they have the legitimate desire to know which men and in what conditions they will obey.

At the same time, two senses of liberty—indicated by Hayek but subordinated to the fundamental notion of non-constraint—inevitably reappear. If there are some men who do not hesitate, in a situation of necessity, to sacrifice individual liberty to the nation's freedom, we would be wrong to deny that they have intelligible motives, if not rational ones, for the preference. As long as there are wars, belonging to a political order will be equivalent to discriminating between friends and enemies. If I have to pay for the liberty I enjoy during peacetime with the obligation of fighting with brothers of the same race, or language, or nationality during war, I can resign myself, with perfect lucidity, to the loss of my peacetime freedom in order to find myself once again among my brothers the day each of us confronts death.

I do not mean to suggest that this is the origin of the nationalistic passion manifested by all peoples for a century, and of the relative indifference towards individual liberty evidenced by many millions of men. It is legitimate to claim that most often nationalism is a scarcely civilized form of tribal consciousness, while, on the contrary, concern for individual liberty marks a later stage of political consciousness. These remarks do not even aim to sketch a sociological interpretation of two sorts of liberty (individual and national). They aim simply at establishing the following proposition: since, as a matter of fact, both in peace and war men are always governed by other men, it is normal and reasonable that the governed *do not* have the sentiment of being free, as soon as they do not belong to the political unit of their choice, of their race or of their language, even if in times of peace the laws leave them a sphere of personal decision.

The same argument holds for liberty defined as participation in the process by which governors are chosen. If, because of the federative power, the latter dispose of the power of life and death over us, is it not quite understandable that we would consider as essential participation, however indirect, in their selection? Whether it has to do with laws or specific commands, the sentiment of obeying oneself depends upon the relation which exists between the citizen and the legislator, between the chief and the soldier. Hayek would be able to meet this objection if he had discovered an objective definition of constraint, a definition which did not take into account what transpires in the consciousness of the related individuals. But, since Hayek himself introduced the notion of threat—constraint is equivalent to the threat of sanctions—the state of mind of both him who commands and him who obeys is part of the very notion of liberty (negation of constraint).

Threat is necessary when the citizen does not spontaneously obey, does not recognize the legitimacy of the authority or the rationality of the order given. The individual will have the sentiment of being oppressed, he will effectively be oppressed (subject to constant threats) insofar as he does not take the state, or the regime, or the governors to be legitimate.

Hayek's goal was philosophically to ground a theory of liberty which would justify reducing to a minimum state intervention in the private sphere, and the maximum enlargement of this sphere. In order to attain this goal he sought an objective definition of constraint (becoming the instrument of another) and decreed that there is a radical opposition between a general law (comparable to a law of nature) and a specific command. But he does not remain firmly attached to his strictly objective definition since he invokes threats. Now, from the moment when states of consciousness have to be taken into consideration, liberty no longer simply depends upon non-intervention of other men in the private sphere. On the other hand, if law, no matter how general, nonetheless expresses the will of certain men, if the governors, holders of the federative power, impose upon citizens the consequences of their decisions, then the rule of law perhaps remains an ideal in certain ways but it cannot be fully realized. All power includes some element of the government of men by men; liberty is not adequately defined by sole reference to the rule of law: the manner in which those who hold this power are chosen, as well as the way in which they exercise it, are felt, in our day, as integral parts of liberty. Wrongly or rightly, men judge themselves free or not according to the nationality of those who legislate and not only according to the relative mixture of laws and specific commands in the conduct of society.

Perhaps the final reason for what I take to be the insufficiency of the philosophy elaborated by Hayek to found his liberalism is his refusal to take into consideration the problem of interior liberty. Hayek, who, on so many points, opposes positivistic tendencies and reproaches Kelsen for having granted the dignity of law to no-matter-what system of statist norms, still allowed himself to be so impressed by a current school of philosophy that he believes that the so-called metaphysical controversies over liberty are devoid of sense.[19] Without entering into this metaphysical controversy, let us note that Hayek quite rightly links liberty with responsibility. He alone can claim liberty who can be held responsible for his actions, and thus is capable of acting rationally:

> The assigning of responsibility thus presupposes the capacity on men's part for rational action, and it aims at making them act more rationally than they would otherwise. It presupposes a certain minimum capacity

in them for learning and foresight, for being guided by a knowledge of the consequences of their actions.[20]

It seems to me less easy than Hayek seems to believe to determine which human beings in fact meet these requirements. At what age do infants cease to be "irresponsible"? At what level of education can a people living under a tribal regime claim no longer to be treated as irresponsible? In other words, within a society the distinction between the "responsible" and the "irresponsible" is not so clear. Likewise, is a so-called civilized society authorized not to recognize and grant the rights of liberty to the members of a so-called archaic society? Hayek's theory presupposes men who have received an education which renders them worthy of liberty. But in each epoch actual politics involve an element of education: should one consider education as constraint? At what point does the education necessary for rationality become a way of refusing to grant men the right to their own mistakes? Within collectivities, just as between tribes or peoples, men have not stopped themselves from imposing upon others, by force, threat or prestige, systems of values or ideas. Hayek correctly writes that "a free society will function successfully only if the individuals are in some measure guided by common values."[21] He sees in this the explanation of the fact that philosophers sometimes have defined liberty as "action conformed to moral laws." It seems to me that Hayek is mistaken when he explains as he does the equivalence, maintained by a thousand philosophers, between morality (or rationality, or universality) and liberty. It suffices to oppose passion and reflection, or animality and consciousness, in order for (interior) liberty to appear as the goal of the effort by which the human animal arrives at his humanity.

Defining liberty by the morality of one's conduct is not without its danger: in the name of the exigencies of education, the one who claims to be invested with a mission will seek to restrict those who think otherwise than he. But danger exists on the other side, too. No collectivity can attain existence and consciousness, i.e., with respect to common values, without an education which often makes people toe the line. The ideal of a society in which each one would be able to choose his gods or his values cannot flourish before its individuals are educated in the common life. Hayek's philosophy presupposes, as already acquired, results which past philosophers considered as the primary objects of political action. In order to leave everyone a private sphere of decision and choice, it is still necessary that all or most want to live together and recognize the same system of ideas as true, the same formulation of legitimacy as valid. A society must first be, before it can be free.

The distinction between liberty and coercion, the foundation of this philosophy, has its origin in reflection on economic behavior. The economic subject, left to himself, freely employs, that is, by choosing his goals and means, the resources he disposes of. On the contrary, individuals subject to a plan risk being degraded into wheels in a mechanism, into mere instruments of "planners." Beginning from a similar analysis, M. Jacques Rueff drew a distinction between two modes of state action.[22] Constraint, he said, always consists in the modification of the desirability or undesirability of an act by modifying its consequences:

> The intervention of the constraining authority modifies by additional desirabilities or undesirabilities the consequences of acts, leads the constrained person to will voluntarily the acts chosen for it by the constraining authority.[23]

Therefore, writes M. Rueff, "the governed man is always left in the hands of his own counsel, he remains a free man." And, "though the coercee still chooses, the alternatives are determined for him by the coercer so that he will choose what the coercer wants."[24]

Constraint, i.e., the modification of individual preferences by sanctions (rewards and punishment), constitutes an inevitable element of government in civilized societies, but this constraint with respect to the rights individual owners possess can be exercised in two ways:

> The government need not affect at all the control that rights-bearers exercise over the domain left to them. Their sovereign domain is lessened by the rights transferred to the government, but after the levying of taxes, the rest remains solely subject to the will of the owner. The latter therefore remains entirely free within his domain. It is for this reason that the form of the corresponding government is called liberal. The second method does not modify the boundaries of the domains of sovereign individuals, but it does impose upon the property owners the necessity of willing the content and usage necessary to accomplish the mission of the government.[25]

The government which forbids an owner of a field from planting a certain crop already excessively available proceeds in this manner.

Both Hayek and Rueff consider individuals acting as economic science conceives them. Each individual chooses and remains, in all circumstances, in the hands of his own counsel. However, remaining on the plane of sociological theory, M. Rueff distinguishes two methods of government, liberal and authoritarian, then two ideal types of society, individualistic and communist, in accordance with whether governmental power fully respects the rights of owners or, on the contrary, denies them all right of appropriation. While preferring the liberal method and the individualistic society, M. Rueff admits the necessity of having some recourse to the authoritarian method and he is resigned to an increase in the functions of the state, provided that the increase does not multiple false rights and does not sow disorder. In other words, he draws from his analysis an accusation against the increase much more than against the authoritarian method.

Hayek wanted to pass from coercion—modification of the desirability of acts by sanctions—to a philosophy of liberty by the intermediary of the generality of the laws. The latter forbid, under pain of punishment, this or that conduct, but they leave a margin of choice. They constitute the equivalent of natural laws to which men must adapt themselves, but do not encroach upon the sphere of individual decision. This argument is open to two objections: First, there is no universally valid delimitation of the private sphere. Hayek, against J. S. Mill, rightly recognizes that there is no individual act that is not susceptible of affecting others. On the other hand, individuals can have the sentiment of being oppressed and in fact be oppressed, as defined by Hayek, by general laws.

On the plane of a theory of the good society, Hayek is not wrong to insist upon two ideas which are fundamental, in my eyes as well as his: liberty is, first of all, negative, non-constraint, the preservation of a private sphere; the more that the orders of power are expressed in impersonal rules, the better chance liberty has of being preserved. These two ideas, however, suffice neither to constitute a philosophy of liberty, nor even, in our time, to formulate the criteria of a free society.

At the beginning Hayek insists upon the necessity of a rigorous distinction between liberty (non-coercion) and other notions such as self-government, democracy, power, status. We need not confuse the concepts: participation in the political process or self-government, even though it often is considered as an element of liberty, ought to be separated from it. Likewise, democracy, whether one defines it, like Hayek, as majoritarian rule or by the organization of a peaceful rivalry for the exercise of power, perhaps favors liberty (in general it does), but is not to be confused with it. That an untrained worker who has nothing to sell but his labor power does not have power, that is, cannot satisfy his desires, goes without saying; for all that, he is not the instrument of others. A beggar can enjoy liberty. Finally, if the members of a minority claim equality vis-à-vis a majority which treats them as inferiors—individual equality within the framework of the existing community, like the blacks in the United States, or collective equality by the constitution of an independent community—this claim, surely legitimate, is not equivalent to a claim for liberty.[26]

If, however, one has followed to the end this process of elimination, one should not be surprised that this kind of liberty has been rare throughout history and that today most men still do not subordinate all their aspirations to it nor do they hold it as the unique or supreme criterion of the social order.

The sentiment of liberty will not be proportionate to effective liberty measured in terms of the adopted definition. Whatever the law, the proletarians observed by Marx could not feel any sentiment of liberty because they were deprived of the minimum of power without which the right to choose ends and means becomes purely illusory. For the mass of Moslems of Algeria, the liberty the French law assures them weighs less heavily on them than the humiliation caused by discrimination. At each epoch, in each society, the sentiment of liberty depends upon one circumstance as a matter of priority. It even depends, perhaps, upon the elimination of a certain form of oppression experienced as intolerable. The exigence of a private sphere can constitute the essential content of the demand for liberty, but this is rare in history: men have risen up against the violence done by victors to their beliefs or morals, against the violence done to their faith by inquisitors, against violence done to their dignity by masters who treat them as slaves or less than men, against the misery inflicted upon them by men or fortune.

Even today, as much as it is legitimate to consider both respect for and the enlargement of this sphere as one of the goals, eventually as the primordial goal, of the social order, it is also as unacceptable to refer to this sole criterion in order to judge all actual societies. It may even be wrong to use the same word to express liberation from the police and liberation from hunger. But one is not wrong to hold that it is wrong, in both theory and practice, to refer everything to a sole objective. Men sacrifice a part of their private sphere in order to be governed by brothers of their race, language, or religion, in order to be treated as equals, in order to have a fatherland, even in the hope of escaping misery and poverty.

At this point Hayek would object that he has not justified liberty as such, as an ultimate value, but, on the contrary, he has justified it pragmatically, by its fruit. The primacy of liberty as conceived by liberals, a primacy we have not accepted without reservation on the philosophic level, must it be accepted on the socio-economic plane? Would the society conformable to the ideal of liberals be not only the morally best but also the most productive and efficient?

Personally, I have always found it hard to believe that, by a preestablished harmony, morality and utility fully coincide. I am suspicious of the ruses of reason as much as I am of the virtuosity of economists. I will not deny my admiration for Hayek's argument, but I will reserve my faith. Like Marxists, liberals sometimes have a tendency to believe that the order of the world can reconcile our aspirations with reality. The confidence is not lacking in grandeur. "Allow me, however, to admire, and not to imitate it."

Translated by Paul Seaton
with Daniel Mahoney

Notes

1. J. W. N. Watkins, "Philosophy," in *Agenda for a Free Society*: *Essays on Hayek's* Constitution of Liberty, published by Arthur Seldon (London: Hutchinson, 1961).
2. *Constitution* p. 133.
3. Ibid., p. 134.
4. Ibid., p. 139.
5. Ibid., p. 20.
6. Ibid., p. 14.
7. Ibid., p. 143. Alluding to military service, Hayek writes: "Though compulsory military service, while it lasts, undoubtedly involves severe coercion, and though a lifelong conscript could not be said ever to be free, a predictable limited period of military service certainly restricts the possibility of shaping one's own life less than would, for instance, a constant threat of arrest, resorted to by an arbitrary power to ensure what it regards as good behavior."

This is an interesting text because it does not envisage the limitation of constraint *within* military service. It thus implies that the soldier as such suffers severe constraint. Hayek does not deny the conclusion, however, that certain human and social activities therefore do not *involve* liberty in the sense in which he has defined it.

8. Ibid., p. 135.
9. Ibid., pp. 150–51.
10. Ibid., p. 153.
11. Ibid., p. 156.
12. Ibid., p. 155.
13. Ibid.
14. Ibid., p. 144.
15. Ibid., p. 314.
16. Ibid.
17. Ibid., p. 145.
18. Ibid., p. 263. Hayek writes: "I wish to add here my opinion that, until the protection of individual freedom is much more firmly secured than it is

now, the creation of a world state probably would be a greater danger to the future of civilization than even war."

19. It appears foolhardy to me to claim that the greatest minds have discussed passionately and over so many centuries questions without import, even without sense. I think the following is, therefore, erroneous:

"It appears that the assertion that the will is free has as little meaning as its denial and the whole issue is a phantom problem, a dispute about words in which the contestants have not made clear what an affirmative or a negative answer would imply."

The debate over the significant or insignificant character of the traditional debate over freedom of the will has replaced the latter debate. I don't see any progress.

20. *Constitution*, p. 76.
21. Ibid., p. 80.
22. Jacques Rueff, *L'Ordre Social* (Paris: 1945), 2 vols.
23. Ibid., vol. II, p. 568.
24. *Constitution*, p. 134.
25. Rueff, vol. II, p. 607.
26. Cf. Sir Isaiah Berlin, *Two Concepts of Liberty* (Oxford: 1958).

Part Three

Totalitarianism and Liberty of the Spirit

Introduction

Aron on Arendt and *The Origins of Totalitarianism*

It is tempting—now that communism, the last and most enduring of the great totalitarian ideologies of our century, has collapsed—to treat totalitarianism as if it were of merely historical or antiquarian interest, as something which contemporary democrats need not reflect about at any length or with any sustained seriousness. There are no doubt various explanations for this temptation. There is an unwillingness on the part of some intellectuals and academics to come to grips with their previous inadequate evaluations of and tepid responses to communist totalitarianism. Many remain committed to an underlying historical progressivism which treats the totalitarian phenomenon as a mere episode or parenthesis in an inevitable process culminating in the actualization of democratic and egalitarian values. But such a reflexive dismissal of reflection about totalitarianism as a part of a distant Cold War past ignores the permanent lessons that can and ought to be discerned from the lived experience of totalitarian despotism. There are few better guides for such an investigation than the two great antitotalitarian political thinkers, Raymond Aron and Hannah Arendt.

Aron's sympathetic but critical account of Arendt's *The Origins of Totalitarianism* originally appeared in the French review *Critique* in 1954, as the main section of a review essay on analyses of totalitarianism. That section of the essay was republished as "The Essence of Totalitarianism According to Hannah Arendt" in *Commentaire*, 28 and 29, 1985. The present essay is the first English translation of Aron's review. It should be noted that Aron's review of the first (1951) edition of *The Origins of Totalitarianism* appeared in 1954, eighteen years before the first section of Arendt's book was published in France in 1972. Arendt's book, and her thought as a whole, would not be taken seriously in Paris until the 1980s, that is, until after the full explosive impact of the thought of Alexander Solzhenitsyn and the Eastern European dissidents was felt in Paris. Aron was almost alone in Parisian intellectual circles during the early years of the Cold War in appreciating Arendt's penetrating genealogy and phenomenology of totalitarianism. He recognized, before it became de rigueur, the genius and courage of Hannah Arendt.

But this piece also highlights Aron's important differences with Arendt. Their differences are both stylistic and substantive. Arendt's approach is excessively metaphysical and insufficiently "sociological" according to Aron. She legitimately attempts to capture the essence of totalitarianism but she underestimates its "accidental" features, its linkage to an era of wars and revolutionary frenzy.[1] Her description of totalitarianism is too hopeless and pathetic in tone in large part because she treats its triumph as tragically semipermanent in character. She tends to ignore the "contradictions" which weaken the twin pillars of Soviet totalitarianism, ideology and terror, and which, over time, create pressures for a return to a more normal civic life. She exaggerates the triumph of human irrationality because her (Germanic) metaphysics discounts the reality of an enduring human and social nature that totalitarian regimes cannot completely or finally transform or overcome. Like the very totalitarians that fascinated and horrified her, Arendt was a kind of (albeit pessimistic) historicist.

Adopting a more political and sociological approach, Aron linked the triumph of a revolutionary party, authoritarian bureaucracy, and the frenzied accumulation of capital to our age of total war and massive social dislocations. Never underestimating the ideological character of Soviet totalitarianism (he emphasized, in contrast to Arendt, the Leninist as opposed to essentially Stalinist character of the regime), Aron believed that communist totalitarianism ultimately warred with both the liberal and the democratic aspirations of modern peoples and the requirements of a self-sustaining industrial society, and even with the civic cohesiveness required of any enduring collectivity. In 1954, while unceasingly opposing the mendacity and irrationality of Soviet totalitarianism, Aron quite remarkably predicted its self-destruction. Aron shows that a belief in the distinctiveness and radicality of the totalitarian regime does not entail a historicist belief in its permanence. His analysis reveals the dishonesty in the fashionable sophism that communist *totalitarianism* never really existed because it did not last forever.

Notes

1.   Paradoxically, in her account of the origins of National Socialist totalitarianism, Arendt probably exaggerated its links to traditional imperialism and antisemitism.

The Essence of Totalitarianism According to Hannah Arendt

Raymond Aron

1954

Mme Arendt's book is an important book. Despite its flaws, which are at times irritating, the reader, even if he is ill-willed, feels little by little as though bewitched by the strength and the subtlety of some of its analyses.

Let us first briefly note a few reservations of secondary importance, and then go on to essential matters. The book's title in English, *The Origins of Totalitarianism* (1951), does not correspond to its contents. The author demonstrates precisely that the antisemitism and the imperialism of the late nineteenth century are only in a limited sense the origin of modern totalitarianism. At most one finds there only the seeds of phenomena that were to bloom in our own time. The book is made up of three juxtaposed studies rather than a well-ordered discussion of one and the same problem.

The book's unity stems from the author's style as much as from the real or forged connections among antisemitism, imperialism, and totalitarianism. Historical figures, countries, parties, and events that appear in the book share a familial likeness, much as do Velásquez's children or Daumier's or Goya's personages. Mme Arendt's style resembles Orwell's in *1984*. The mediocrity or inhumanity of all those who play a role in the drama are such that, in the end, one sees the world as the totalitarians present it and one risks feeling mysteriously attracted by the horror or the absurdity that is described. I am not sure that Mme Arendt is not in some way fascinated by the monsters she takes from reality but which her logical imagination, in some respects comparable to the imagination of the ideologues she denounces, brings to their point of perfection.

In order to find the sense or absurdity she seeks, Mme Arendt is often quick to justify in a small stroke, whether true or false, a general proposition which is at the least doubtful. The Dreyfus Affair ended not, as she says, by a decision of the Court of Appeal (page 90), but by a decision of the Court of Cassation. The illegality of this decision is at least open to discussion. Her portrait of Captain Dreyfus (page 91) is borrowed from anti-Dreyfusard writing and, to the best of my knowledge, does not conform to reality. A few lines from his book, *Pleins Pouvoirs*, do not prove that Jean Giraudoux was in complete accord with Petain or the Vichy government on the subject of "nationalist antisemitism" (pages 48–49). The reference to a book written during the war by a Frenchman in the United States does not suffice to prove the anecdote of Maurras' encounter with a female astrologer (page 110) who is said to have invited the old doctrinarian to collaborate with the Germans (which Maurras, moreover, did not do).

These remarks suggest a reproach of a certain gravity. Without even being aware of it, Mme Arendt affects a tone of haughty superiority regarding things and men. She abuses the adjectives "grotesque" and "farcical." She seems to try hard not to see the dramas of conscience that tore men who were Dreyfusards out of concern for truth and conservatives or militarists out of conviction. As interpreted by Mme Arendt, the Dreyfus Affair leaves an equivocal impression on the French reader: an excess of rationalization on the one hand and of disdain for simple mortals on the other makes for the presentation of a grimacing humanity. Picquard and Clemenceau are about the only ones to escape her historian's rigor. English readers have the same difficulty recognizing their country's imperialists in the images Mme Arendt has offered them. The mixture of German metaphysics, subtle sociology, and moral vituperations ends up exaggerating the qualities and the faults of men and of regimes (are all men truly unhappy in a totalitarian regime?), substituting for real history a history that is at every moment ironic or tragic. The Jews are persecuted at the very moment they have lost all real influence; South Africa is conquered at the very moment it no longer holds any strategic worth; superfluous individuals and superfluous capitals go off in quest of that most superfluous of goods, gold. . . . Each one of these theses probably contains an element of truth. But they could be expressed in a way that would remove from each one, through the cunning of reason, a part of the disproportionate credence that Mme Arendt seems ready to give them.

On Antisemitism

The study of antisemitism in the first part of the book is rich in ideas and facts and filled with original perspectives. Particularly notable are the description of the diverse modalities of emancipation, the attitude of the literary circles toward the Jews, and the relations between the banker or parvenu and the "ordinary Jew." But if one is prepared to subscribe to most of the ideas taken separately, neither the organizing concepts nor the ideas which the author in the end sets down as essential are wholly convincing.

Whether it is a matter of antisemitism or imperialism, the decisive social fact would be the intervention of the mob. Mme Arendt sees social classes as groups that are still integrated within a national collectivity and preserving something of the common consciousness of the Estates (*Stände*). The mob would stem from the dissolution of the classes; it would gather scattered individuals without giving them any cohesion. Marx called the proletariat the dissolution of all classes. Mme Arendt would reserve this formulation for the mob. But what is the mob?

The antisemitic crowds who demonstrated in Paris against Zola, or at Rennes against Victor Basch, were in no way homogeneous. Students stood side by side craftsmen or businessmen, and perhaps workers, too. Was the social origin of these crowds fundamentally different from that of the crowds of the revolutions of the first half of the nineteenth century? The sons of the bourgeoisie joined with the bottom rung of society as well to bring down Louis-Philippe as well as to acclaim Louis-Napoleon or Boulanger. In one case, they were the allies of workers; in the other of the petty bourgeois above all, although it would be hard to deny the presence of workers or craftsmen in Bonapartist or Boulangist crowds. On the other hand, in the nineteenth century modern industrial societies already created the proletariat and peasantry, intermediary groups that were outside the recognized classes of the bourgeoisie and which no one has ever known quite how to define or designate precisely. It is hard to tell whether the mob of which Mme Arendt speaks covers the disintegrated individuals who are the inevitable product of the development of industrial society and who would encompass all or part of the intermediary groups, or whether the mob is the name given to all those who by personal failure fall from their class and who then swell the ranks of the rebels. This is not a simple matter of semantics or a quarrel over a definition. In the first instance, the mob comprises, along with those who have failed, those groups which social and economic progress tends spontaneously to dissolve and to place outside the community. In the second instance, the mob is made up exclusively of failures from all classes. Depending on which thesis one accepts, the dissolution of European society appears to be the necessary result of capitalist development or, on the contrary, it can be traced to events, wars, or crises. Mme Arendt seems inclined to the first of these alternatives, but without making a clear choice.

I doubt that individuals who are sensitive to imperialist or antisemitic propaganda belong to a socially delineated group. That is nonetheless what Mme Arendt probably thinks when, in the last part of her book, she defines the masses by the decomposition of the classes and explains the alliance of the elite and the mob by elements common to the one and the other. When ordinary men leave organized groups, they find themselves sensitive to the same sort of ideology and propaganda as do the intellectual rebels against bourgeois morality. "Atomized, isolated individuals" are ruthlessly malleable. But in that sense there was no more mob or mass in Germany than in France before the war of 1914. Underdeveloped industry is not the sole cause of the mob's numerical weakness in France. It is not capitalism as such, but the war of 1914 and the failure of the crash of 1919 that broke up millions of Germans and reduced them to the status of masses.

I also doubt the idea that Mme Arendt develops in the early part of her book, at the beginning, as though it constituted the book's essential contribution. The Jewish tragedy would have occurred at the moment the Jews ceased to fulfill a function in history. It would be wrong for them to rest contented simply with the scapegoat theory. They were struck, as were the French nobles, at the moment when their privileges no longer corresponded to the services they rendered.

I confess that comparing the Jews of the twentieth century to the French aristocracy of the eighteenth century does not convince me. It is true that at the end of the nineteenth century the Jewish bankers were no longer a national and international power that dealt with sovereigns as equals. But it is hard to see how these bankers' loss of power, at a time when they were no longer distinguishable from their Catholic or Protestant colleagues, would have brought them punishment. They possessed no more privileges than the other bankers and their decline did not make them targets of popular condemnation. By contrast, it is easy to explain, in a quite banal way, that the progress of emancipation and assimilation evoked strong reactions in this or that quarter where old prejudices remained to protest against the rise of Jews to positions hitherto closed to them (witness the reaction of certain French Catholics to the appointment of Jewish officers to staff positions). Likewise, in Germany, the sudden influx of Jews from the East into certain professions is one cause of the force of antisemitism in Weimar Germany. On the subject of Austrian antisemitism, Mme Arendt explains perfectly well how it resulted from the very structure of the dualist monarchy, torn by quarrels between nationalities out of which sprang the Pan-Germanist movement which, like all racist movements, denied the traditional nationalism whose simple expression it at first appeared to be.

Drumont's antisemitism, as Bernanos described it, is the expression of a revolt against the triumph of money, against the rise to social prominence of uprooted people who get power and fortune from abstract dealings. Confusedly, the Jews were made responsible for the civilization of money (see, for example, Marx's essay *On the Jewish Question*). The nostalgia for old France, in the writings of some intellectuals and semi-intellectuals, becomes tainted with antisemitism which in turn wins over certain circles that have felt the new competition of the Jews. There is no lack of comparisons between the climate in France twenty years after the proclamation of the Republic and the climate in Germany fifteen years after the establishment of the Republic: discussion regarding the political regime, regret for the old France or the old Germany, the decline of the "great Jews" of old and the rapid assimilation of ordinary Jews, the imputation to these newcomers of certain unpleasant elements of the regime, the instability of things and the precarious nature of the nation's destiny, etc. It is without any artifice that one would invent the simplistic scapegoat theory and the overly subtle theory of antisemitism striking a group that has lost its function and retained its privileges.

The emancipation of the Jews followed the progress of liberal ideas, and the liberals played a part in the fulfillment of the nationalist idea. As long as nationalism was dominant, antisemitism did not pass beyond the limits of its French modalities, which were reactionary, one might say traditional, what Maurras called state antisemitism. Antisemitism does not become racism until nationalism reaches its climax and at the same time denies itself in imperialism which, among the Germans of Austria-Hungary, finds its expression in Pan-Germanism and not in vague desires for overseas conquests. The rights of man were accorded the Jews because they were granted to all men inasmuch as they were men. In 1871, Renan wrote to David Strauss that the annexation of the Alsatians against their explicit will opened the way to "zoological wars." The argument no doubt accorded with the French claim and one could have objected, from the other side of the Rhine, that the "Francization" of Alsace had been undertaken by violence ever since the end of the seventeenth century. But Renan nonetheless formulated a true and profound idea: as soon as nationality was no longer considered the result of a decision freely taken by men but rather as a datum of nature, the two elements of the liberal movement—the rights of man and the rights of nations to sovereign independence—had to come apart. This was a regression to a tribal nationalism and the individual no longer existed save in and by his nation and had no rights save within his own nation. The unification of national groupings became a supreme objective. Such a turn of events explains how the Jew could be dehumanized in the eyes of Hitler's party, once he was expelled from the community of race or tribe.

The rights of man were founded on a religious conception of the person or on a humanist conception of individual conscience. One could inquire what their foundation would be in a naturalist philosophy. Yet, on the other hand, at the very time when European men appealed to them, they did not extend their benefit to all other men. Germany, Great Britain, and France recognized each other as states. In other words, they did not plan to destroy each other in the event of war. Germans, Frenchmen, Englishmen traveled throughout old Europe without passports. But how were the Negroes of the Congo treated? The European states would not have hesitated to divide the Chinese empire among themselves and refuse to grant it existence as a state, if circumstances had lent themselves to such actions. The materialist philosophers of the last century were more often than not humanitarians. While believers in the rights of man did not apply their belief logically to all men, the naturalists could have succeeded in recognizing the humanity of their fellow men, although their philosophy was incapable of grounding the humanity of the individual who was excluded from every community. Racist ideology alone does not account for the deed which remains enormous, monstrous: the killing of six million Jews. . . .

The Essence of Totalitarianism

In the first two parts of her book, Mme Arendt writes as a historian and a sociologist. She multiplies explanations for events in accord with their circumstances. We are inclined to accept her explanations in their particulars rather than as a whole. In the book's third part, her method changes. Totalitarianism is not to be explained by social or economic data. It is rather a regime, one unprecedented in history whose essence itself needs to be grasped. In order to understand the behavior of Hitlerians and Stalinists, one must grasp their ideology and not allow oneself to be taken with shallow pragmatic interpretations. The requisitioning of means of transportation in view of the extermination of the Jews during wartime is absurd if the primary goal is to win victory. The collectivization of agriculture in the USSR is absurd in light of the fact that it entails the destruction of half the livestock and the catastrophic reduction of crops. Concentration camps are absurd in view of production efficiency.

These very examples bring to the fore a question that recurs in a variety of forms. In a sense, Mme Arendt is right. The pragmatic interpretation of totalitarian behavior is indeed erroneous, but this is so because we forget the system of values or passions held by the actors. Extermination was indeed a war objective of the Hitlerites. Perhaps they wished to attain it even before the end of hostilities so that in any event, their hatred might be satisfied.

However, more serious doubts arise regarding the Soviet examples Mme Arendt gives. The collectivization of agriculture became irrational because of peasant resistance. But at least collectivization had a rational motive: increased yields. The planners could not seduce the peasants with higher prices. To do that would have required consumer goods which planned industrial output did not make possible. The irrationality of the labor camps, too, is more open to debate than Mme Arendt contends. In any case, forced labor does not appear irrational to planners because of the very possibilities it offers.

But let us suppose these theses to be true. Is Hitlerism essentially the universe of the S.S., of the gas chambers, of extermination commandos? Are the ravages of collectivization or the labor camps the essence of industrial construction? Mme Arendt replies with confidence: they are the *essence*.

Totalitarian regimes are defined neither alone by the suppression of representative institutions and multiple parties, nor by the absolute power of a team or a man. The regimes of the colonels in Poland, of Franco in Spain, even of Mussolini belong to a species of which history offers many examples. Fascism holds little or no originality. The single party occupies the place of a police force, aids in the recruitment of upper- and middle-level administrators, gathers together the leader's principal partners and makes it possible for them to reap the rewards of their complicity, and offers an access to certain union or government positions for young people seeking them. Up to the time of its alliance with Hitler, fascism contained no trace of antisemitism or of permanent revolution. To the very end, it did not shake the traditional structure of Italian society.

Totalitarianism seems to be characterized by a certain number of institutional phenomena that Mme Arendt analyzes admirably: the proliferation of bureaucracies, poorly linked to one another in an inextricable tangle of official spheres; the split between the party of the masses and the inner circle; the maintenance of a kind of conspiracy within the party that controls the state; the unconditioned authority of the leader, who is indispensable less for any uncommon administrative or intellectual virtues than for his ability to resolve conflicts among his comrades or among the innumerable agencies; the expansion of a secret police that becomes the supreme power; the police state locking arms with an obsessional ideological propaganda addressed to the masses; and the development of an esoteric doctrine reserved for the few. No one of these phenomena in particular reveals the originality of totalitarianism. *All of them taken together* reveals its essence, named by terms such as "permanent revolution" or "terror and ideology."

Many times, in phases of revolutionary crisis, the demands of ideological orthodoxy have manifested themselves. The novelty does not lie in the fact that the communist party, once it seized power, sought to put aside individuals, groups, and agencies. The novelty lies in the communist party's holding more sway in 1938 than in 1917, more in 1952 than in 1938. The ideological passion does not abate; rather it is exacerbated. Stalin's Marxism is more all-encompassing than Lenin's. No one in the 1920s would have conceived of anything like the condemnation of genetics.

In the same way, totalitarian terror intensifies over time. It is fully unleashed when the regime has no more adversaries. The great purge that imprisoned between five and seven million citizens, among them key figures in technical and military spheres, took place in 1937–38, at a time when peasant resistance had been broken and when the initial difficulties of the industrial buildup had been overcome. *Terror* is the essence of the totalitarian regime, terror manifest in hitherto unknown ways. From the moment punishment is meted out to a potential criminal, whose action may have been harmful to the Revolution, or to one who, by belonging to a group condemned by history, may be harmful tomorrow, from the moment whole categories of people are singled out, everyone feels abandoned, alone. While the party's collective dynamism moves ahead, individuals become frantic or resigned, prisoners of an implacable fatality, the playthings of an inhuman force.

Once abandoned, individuals lose the organic ties that bind them to their families, their neighbors, their companions at work or in poverty. The wife or children seek the father's death; no one any longer trusts his neighbor; the secret police are present in every factory, every office, even within every home. This "massification" reaches its extreme form in the camps, where the individual is anonymous, lost in the midst of a crowd where fertile solitude is forbidden. The camp management regulates the life of these phantoms who pass from an existence of shades on to death, without anyone sensing the event as human or meaningful.

The Third Reich, according to Mme Arendt, did not become totalitarian until the last phase of the war, at the time when the genocide was consummated and Himmler was monopolizing power as minister of the Interior, chief of police, commander of the home army, and so on. During Hitler's fifteen years in power, the regime was a mixed one, in which traditional elements—the army, management, the economy—limited the activity of those who in the Third Reich were called fanatical Hitlerites. Mme Arendt's thesis is that these "fanatics" are the core of the movement, the embodiment of its historical essence, who were not destined to give way to the moderates, but who on the contrary had allied themselves with the moderates to allay suspicion. They had camouflaged themselves as nationalists in order to seduce the philistines they despised. In the wake of victory, they would have reigned at last and so transformed the social map of Europe and extended the technique of genocide to Slavic peoples. The fanatics did indeed win out during the war, but it can be argued that this happened because of the force of circumstances, without asserting with any certainty what would have happened in the case of a military victory for the Third Reich.

Stalinist Totalitarianism

With regard to Stalinist totalitarianism, Mme Arendt limits herself to indicating that it has nothing to do with Lenin, who, quite to the contrary, would have attempted to give the Russian masses an undifferentiated structure (page 312). Likewise, she indicated that totalitarianism had nothing to do with Marxism. It could have arisen only in the 1930s. Let us recapture a few banal statements among these profound observations.

The primary, but not the solely sufficient condition of a totalitarian regime is the seizure of power by a party that assures itself a monopoly of politics. This condition was attained in Lenin's own time, thanks to Lenin himself. The Bolsheviks, a minority party surrounded by enemies, took from the old regime its police, which, thanks to the civil war, had achieved a stature and acquired power greater than it possessed in the last days of a weakened Czarism. In Lenin's own lifetime, the opposition parties, including the socialist and revolutionary parties, were outlawed. Marxism was not called into question, any more than was the equation of the party's power with proletariat power. More than that, the basis for all lies was set down: according to

Marxist doctrine, the socialist revolution ought to have succeeded capitalist expansion, the institutions of socialist society should have been present at the heart of the old society. In face of what actually happened, Lenin's acceptance of Trotsky's thesis that it was not impossible to jump over the bourgeois and capitalist phase was at the origin of the equivocating called "socialist construction," the industrial development phase that Marxist theory itself considered to be the proper function of capitalism. Until 1923, the discrepancy between ideology and reality was not so blatant because neither civil war and wartime communism nor the N.E.P. (New Economic Policy) was referred to as "socialist construction." Lenin nonetheless created the indispensable conditions for the permanent substitution of ideology for reality, in which Mme Arendt rightly sees one of the characteristic traits of Stalinism.

What did the totalitarian regime need in order to flourish? The gap between reality and ideology had to show itself. In other words, the accelerated development of production forces in accord with forced savings and planning had to arouse phenomena comparable to those found in Western Europe at the same economic stage (though these phenomena worsened in the USSR). At the same time, Power had to maintain and to amplify the ideological system of interpretation which was made to stand as official truth. When Stalin took over from the leftist opposition the industrialization program which it had formulated, he took it upon himself to impose upon a recalcitrant people a considerable austerity program in order to finance investments and also to require that the peasants produce grain without receiving consumer goods in return. The need to increase yields and the doctrinaire concern to destroy every class founded upon private ownership brought on the politics of collectivization. This led to the fierce repression of peasant resistance, the temporary ruin of agriculture, the slaughtering of livestock, and famine. The kind of civil war that came with the construction of factories and collective farms no doubt went on being serenely baptized as "socialist construction." Inevitably, the logical and murderous folly that to Mme Arendt appears as the essence of totalitarianism kept on gaining ground. The party had to be transformed into an impeccably disciplined instrument made to believe, on orders from above, that it was daylight in the dead of night, and to recognize socialism in these tragic events of first-phase industrialization. One needed an absolute faith in the Party, in History, and in humanity's fulfillment in a classless society, in order to combine cynicism in one's actions with a kind of long-range idealism.

However, one could say that although circumstances can explain the totalitarianism of 1930–1934, they do not explain the great purge of 1936–1938. And therein lies Mme Arendt's main argument: that circumstances do not account for Stalinism's totalitarian terror, since such terror increases just when it has become rationally useless. The argument is forceful, set against superficial and erroneously objective books such as Isaac Deutscher's, who seeks a comprehensive explanation of totalitarian phenomena in terms of socio-economic circumstances. In spite of everything, the victims of the great purge have sought to account for the phenomenon whose victims they were. Without reproducing here the sixteen theories presented by Beck and Godin[1] (pseudonyms of a physician of Austrian extraction and a Russian historian who met in a Soviet prison), some of them at least suggest interpretations that make the repression partially intelligible, however absurd its excessiveness.

The hierarchical, inegalitarian, despotic society that came out of the five-year plans bore no resemblance to the image fashioned aforehand by the revolutionaries. There could be no resemblance because, according to the very theory that subordinates social organization to forces of production, a sufficient development of the latter was the indispensable condition of socialist benefits. Since the development of the means of production, deceptively baptized socialism, required still many more five-year plans, idealists who would never be reconciled to this fact had to be eliminated. Starting from this discrepancy between ideology and reality, other theories were elaborated: the scapegoat theory (responsibility for failures and hardships should be laid on the privileged few); the testing theory (party members must blindly accept any decision, even one that strikes them, in order to accomplish the indispensable transfer of loyalty from the idea to the party); the theory of Caesarean mania for persecution (how could the government not be in anguish when it knows it is lying and knows that the masses know it and know that it knows they know); and so on.

There is more, however. Reality itself to some extent requires terror. A fundamental contradiction gnaws at the socialist buildup, that is, at industrialization under the impetus of the state. If it is legal and moderate, state-controlled and bureaucratic initiative cannot be favorable to the increase of production and to productivity. It can only be made to work through the method of the Pharaohs or by appeal to individual interest. The recruitment of forced laborers is the ultimate form which the builders' indifference to means and human resources takes, provided that goals are attained. In the bureaucratic framework, on the other hand, technicians or managers are the pioneers. They must make the plan work and they only succeed by using clandestine networks that spawn on the fringe of legal channels. They determine to do so because it is no less risky for them to remain within the bounds of law than to transgress it. Terror is perhaps indispensable to avoid a bureaucratic petrification that would obstruct the achievement of the paradoxical task of developing means of production under state impetus. Were the regime to become stabilized, a hierarchical bureaucracy would appear, resembling in its exterior forms the Ch'in dynasty, and henceforth encompassing an industrial rather than a predominantly agricultural society.

Is it possible to give the bureaucratic bourgeoisie, that product of industrialization, all the advantages it already possesses (high salaries, non-graduated income taxes, educational benefits to children) and as well personal security and stable employment? Such stability would slow down production. Given the age at which, in the 1920s and 1930s, those bourgeoisie came to occupy top positions, it would allow dissatisfaction to be concentrated on irremovable managers and would give them an authority and confidence that would progressively limit the party's omnipotence. The party maintains social mobility while it is at the same time the only outcome of conflicts within a ruling class that has not yet established the constitutional procedures by which to regulate conflicts peaceably.

All these explanations, even when they are combined, leave us with a mysterious margin: the mass arrest of millions of people that crippled industries, the army, and the managerial elite was neither necessary nor reasonable. It is not certain that anyone wanted the great purge as it actually unfolded, any more than anyone wanted collectivization as it was practiced. The snowball mechanism described in Weissberg's admirable book[2] may have intervened as much as Stalin's sadism did.

Ideology and Terror

These sociological explanations, sketched quickly here, are by no means incompatible with Mme Arendt's interpretations which seek out the essence of totalitarianism. The complex connections which she establishes among terror, ideology, and the police do not vanish on account of these explanations. It is not out of the question to consider terror the essence of the totalitarian regime in order to distinguish it from simple tyranny which is the absolute power of one only, ruling over all and reducing them to impotence. But the totalitarian essence did not arise mysteriously, fully armed, out of the mind of History or out of the mind of Stalin. Certain circumstances favored its emergence, and others will foster its disappearance.

In an article entitled "Ideology and Terror" written for the Karl Jaspers Festschrift,[3] Mme Arendt articulates both her method and her thought by recourse to Montesquieu's ideas. Every political regime has a nature and a principle. The nature is "that which makes a thing be what it is and the principle is what makes it act." The monarchical principle is honor; the republican is virtue. Tyranny's principle is terror. However, Mme Arendt goes on to say that totalitarianism has no principle. A regime whose ideology proclaims cosmic or historical laws superior to the will of human beings, whose praxis throws individuals into isolation and abandonment and prepares them to accept the roles of executioner or victim is not even moved by fear. In order for fear to move anyone to act, the individual must believe that by his action he escapes the threats of repression or purge. Totalitarianism is an attempt to exercise a total domination of men which dehumanizes them, either by sending them to concentration camps or, in so-called normal society, by subjecting them to obsessive propaganda and to mysterious decisions made by authorities who themselves appeal to cosmic and human laws.

One cannot help asking whether, formulated in this way, Mme Arendt's thesis is not contradictory. A regime without a principle is not a regime. It cannot be compared to either a monarchy or a republic. As a regime, it exists only in its creator's imagination. In other words, Mme Arendt constitutes an essentially political regime out of certain aspects of Hitlerite and Stalinist phenomena. She brings out and probably exaggerates the originality of German and Russian totalitarianism. Taking this genuine originality as the equivalent of a fundamental regime, she is led to see in our time the negating of traditional philosophies. And she slides toward a contradiction: defining a functioning regime by an essence that implies the impossibility of functioning.

In one sense, the ideology and terror of totalitarianism are the amplification of revolutionary phenomena, a connection made by Crane Brinton in *The Anatomy of Revolution*.[4] As has often been said, the Bolsheviks are Puritans or Jacobins who succeeded, that is, who held on to power. They too say or think that only the pure will save the Revolution. They too, once they embody that state, reject the liberty they demanded of their enemies in power. They too are the apostles of "the despotism of liberty," a logical contradiction which a historian can easily explain since social upheavals in their first phase exclude democratic methods, even if they are to be ultimately favorable to democracy. A revolutionary society imposes on its militants a break with all other bonds. Nothing, neither family nor work, matters in the face of the true faith—in God or in the classless society—and of authentic action for individual or collective salvation. To the extent that this attitude and these beliefs are maintained, the common man in effect finds himself, according to Mme Arendt's analysis, sacrificed to mysterious laws, severed from closeknit communities, subjected to a terror that merges not only with the arbitrary will of one man, but also with a sort of fatality.

One could say that revolutionary fever, as Crane Brinton analyzes it, cannot last for as long as several decades. Yet, indeed, Bolshevism is taking on patent, even radical newness by comparison with other revolutionary societies. Aiming beyond the goals of Puritans or Jacobins, situating the Promised Land at the end of historical development, promising economic equality and abundance for all, Bolshevism entails and justifies a prolonged revolution as it baptizes the development of the means of production to be "socialist construction." The accumulation of capital or technical Westernization under the direction of a revolutionary sect entails this mixture of terror and ideology characteristic of the rule of extremists.

At the same time, socialist construction under state impetus follows upon a Russian tradition—the Communist party is a collective Peter the Great, as Elie Halévy put it—and reestablishes a bureaucracy that is at once managerial and technical, far more extensive by contrast with the Czarist bureaucracy. Little by little, the Stalinist bureaucracy guarantees itself material advantages, prestige, external signs of hierarchy, and imitations of traditional bureaucracy. To the benefit of the party's secretary general, the secular religion of revolutionary ideology ends up playing the same role that orthodox religion did for the czars. Caesaro-papism is reborn and the interpreter of History becomes the pope-emperor.

Essence and Duration of Totalitarianism

The totalitarian phenomenon thus entails many interpretations because it has many causes. The method that aims at grasping its essence is legitimate, but on condition that it does not neglect complementary methods. Otherwise, one cannot raise what is perhaps the most important question: for how long a time is totalitarianism destined to last? Is it the temporary and pathological accompaniment of certain transformations? Or is it, despite its intrinsic absurdity, susceptible of prolonging itself in a kind of permanent dehumanization of human societies? In *1984*, George Orwell suggested a sociological thesis: the single party, the authoritarian bureaucracy, the state orthodoxy, the

investment plans and privations imposed on all, the psychological con-
ditioning of the victims—all of these are susceptible to forging a system compatible with industrial society. While progress in productivity
would make it possible for the first time in history for a higher culture to be founded without the misery of the greatest number, the
totalitarian regime encourages war and despotism, reserving once again
the profits of civilization for the few alone. In this case, totalitarianism would not be connected with a phase of build-up or attributable
to the weight of a specifically Russian past, but it would be the polit-
ico-ideological superstructure of a modern planned economy.

In a contrary view, Isaac Deutscher in his last book decrees that
Stalinist barbarity was the more or less inevitable method by which
Russian barbarity was dispelled and that it will not survive the country's technical Westernization. By its works, Stalinism would destroy
its own foundation. There are several objections to raise against both
Deutscher's thesis and the way he demonstrates it. Yet, the decisive
question has been raised: does not the industrialization of society itself tend to erode the foundations of Stalinism? More than anything
else, I want to delineate a distinction that is implicit in Mme Arendt's
book, between bureaucratic despotism and economic planning on the
one hand, and totalitarianism (that is, ideology and terror) on the other. Economic progress tends of itself to eliminate or attenuate the latter; but in no way does it exclude the former.

As the social elite's intellectual level rises and a democratic bourgeoisie becomes stabilized, terrorism and ideological fanaticism will
be more and more difficult to maintain because they will go against
the people's spontaneous aspirations and because a party that is in-
creasingly recruited from among the technical elite and privileged
people inevitably loses the purity and fanaticism of a sect. On the other
hand, bureaucratic despotism remains the most useful superstructure
of a totally planned economy of the Soviet type. It is doubtful that
election procedures could be introduced in such a regime, unless there
will be an unforeseen increase in available resources. But an authoritarian bureaucracy cannot do completely without an ideology to justify itself, and such an ideology always carries the risk of reviving
revolutionary crises.

A more thorough analysis would have to take a number of factors
into account: will one of Stalin's successors succeed in making himself the absolute leader, that is, succeed in eliminating his rivals or in
convincing the masses that he is in the process of eliminating his rivals? How will the international conflict evolve? How will the Chinese revolution affect Russia's regime? Too many different elements

are involved, too many accidents or too many people can intervene to allow predictions to be formulated. Totalitarian phenomena, as we have known them in the first half of the twentieth century, have been linked simultaneously to a revolutionary party, to an authoritarian bureaucracy, and to drastic happenings such as war or the frenzied accumulation of capital. We have not yet experienced a totalitarian revolution's return to normal life. This lack of experience calls for prudence in making predictions. It does not forbid us from hoping that there might be an outcome other than apocalyptic catastrophe to the furors of the abandoned masses and faithless quasi-intellectuals.

It would be wrong to insist that human irrationality has won the day once and for all.

Translated by Marc LePain
with Daniel Mahoney

Notes

1. See F. Beck and W. Godin, *Russian Purge and the Extraction of Confession* (New York: Viking Press, 1951).

2. A. Weissberg, *L'Accusé*, preface by Arthur Koestler (Paris: Fasquelle, 1953).

3. This chapter appears as the final chapter of the revised editions of *The Origins of Totalitarianism*, beginning in 1958. (Editor's note)

4. Crane Brinton, *The Anatomy of Revolution* (New York: Prentice-Hall, 1952).

Introduction

Sartre and Solzhenitsyn

Aron characteristically defines his political position in opposition to the more "literary" politics of Jean-Paul Sartre, who asserts that politics is of no interest if the amelioration and mitigation of the defects of social life is the only course available to political men.

For those, like Sartre, infected by the revolutionary or historicist virus, the political perspective is strangely unintelligible. From the perspective of historicism, the political perspective, expecting no radical mutation in the nature of social and political life, looks like nothing so much as a Sisyphean enterprise to improve the intrinsically unimprovable. The Marxist or revolutionary historicist, blind to political reasoning, easily confuses political moderation with unmanly nihilistic resignation. As Aron argued in *The Opium of the Intellectuals*, the rejection of the political perspective by Sartre and others necessarily entails a strange fusion of absolutism and relativism. Revolutionary intellectuals desiring a radical change in the essence of the human condition soon are forced by their futile project to indulge in the relativistic defense of the "lie" surrounding the totalitarian practice of "the Revolution."

Despite his enduring political differences with Sartre and his recognition of Sartre's fundamental and never acknowledged nor much less repudiated political irresponsibility, Aron had great respect for talents of his "petit camarade" from the Ecole Normale Supérieure. In many of his writings, most prominently his *Memoirs*, Aron seems dogged by a nagging suspicion that his own achievements, however much in accord with the requirements of truth and responsibility, are of a lesser standing than that of the more "original," "literary," and "creative" work of his youthful friend and longtime intellectual adversary.

If Aron's work is sometimes characterized by undue or exaggerated respect for Sartre's achievement and by an excessive and some-

113

what self-deceptive intellectual modesty, this cannot be said of his 1976 contribution to a festschrift for his old friend, the Austrian ex-communist and distinguished novelist Manès Sperber, entitled "Alexander Solzhenitsyn and European 'Leftism.'" In this short, spirited, and morally invigorating polemic, Aron contrasts the worlds of the "European Leftist," represented above all by Sartre, smug in his dogmatic rejection of traditional categories of good and evil and oblivious to the "lie" at the heart of the communist enterprise, and that of the "Soviet" dissident, Alexander Solzhenitsyn, whose personal experience of the evil of ideology has led him to recognize, and witness to, the enduring reality of the "age-old distinction between good and evil." Despite important political and philosophical differences with Solzhenitsyn, Aron retained a profound admiration for the fundamental message of the *zek* turned writer and moral witness. Solzhenitsyn added great moral weight and authority, a kind of existential verification to that which Sartre had obstinately denied and Aron had ceaselessly affirmed: "There is something worse than poverty and repression— and that something is the Lie; the lesson this century teaches us is to recognize the deadly snare of ideology, the illusion that men and social organizations can be transformed at a strike."

At the end of this essay, Aron criticizes the "unrepentant ideologues" who dominate the press, radio, and television of the Western democracies. It is tempting to consider such a judgment both somewhat overstated and a bit passé, given the sudden collapse of communist regimes and the concomitant discrediting of "fellow traveling" or moral indulgence toward these regimes. Yet in the *The New York Times Book Review* of January 10, 1993, a distinguished critic writes *à propos* of a recent book chronicling and criticizing the political irresponsibility of Sartre and other fellow-traveling French intellectuals after World War II:

> [S]hould we demand that intellectuals always be responsible? . . . we do not have to share a single one of Sartre's intellectual or political opinions in order to defend his right to have aired and argued for them and to have been as irresponsible as he liked.

Given the present international political situation, "fellow traveling" is no longer a tenable (that is, respectable) political option for the antibourgeois critic or intellectual. But remarkably and distressingly, the spirit of "Sartrism," with its contempt for the very categories of prudential judgment and moral good and evil, persists with only slightly diminished influence in the intellectual and academic world.

Alexander Solzhenitsyn and European "Leftism"

Raymond Aron

1976

Some time ago I read three articles in the *Nouvel Observateur* in which Jean-Paul Sartre gave what seemed to be a self-portrait in the form of answers to questions put by his friend Contat; I also read, more or less simultaneously, Solzhenitsyn's *The Oak and the Calf.* On page 119 Solzhenitsyn refers to an encounter, which in the event did not take place, between the greatest contemporary Russian writer and the man whom he calls the "ruler of minds" in the West. I trust the reader will forgive me for reproducing Solzhenitsyn's account of this episode word for word:

> Six months later the man whose canvassing obtained the prize for Sholokhov (and inflicted the most hurtful insult imaginable on Russian literature)—Jean Paul Sartre—was in Moscow, and through his interpreter expressed a wish to see me. I met the interpreter on Mayakovsky Square, and she told me that "the Sartres were expecting me to dine with them at the Peking Hotel." At first sight it might seem well worth my while to meet Sartre: here was a "master of men's minds" in France and throughout Europe, an independent writer with a worldwide reputation. There was no reason why we should not be sitting together around a table in ten minutes' time: I could complain about all the things that had been done to me, and this wandering minstrel of humanism would alert all Europe. If only it had been someone other than Sartre. Sartre needed me partly to satisfy his curiosity, partly so that he would have the right later on to talk about our meeting, perhaps to criticize me— and I would have no means of defending myself. I said to the interpreter: "What's the good of two writers meeting if one of them is gagged and has his hands tied behind his back?"
> "Aren't you interested in meeting him?"
> "It would be unbearably painful. My head is barely above water. Let him help us to get published first."
> I drew an analogy between Russian literature and the deformed boy in *Cancer Ward*. It seemed to me just as twisted and one-sided when

115

viewed from Europe. The undeveloped potential of our great literature
has remained completely unrecognized there.

I wonder whether Sartre discerned in my refusal the depth of our
aversion to him?[1]

For an answer to this question we have only to open Simone de
Beauvoir's latest book. Lena reports to the "Sartres" that Solzhenitsyn
does not wish to meet them. "Why not?" asks Simone de Beauvoir.
Solzhenitsyn had not made himself clear. And she adds: "We are surprised at his reaction. There can be no doubt that Sartre knew him
better than he knew Sartre."

Which of them knew the other better? Sartre, who leads the life of
a student loafer in Paris, drifting from café to café, and who travels
the world unhindered and esteemed? Or Solzhenitsyn, hounded by the
police, after years in camp, years of exile? The one has at his disposal all the information which press and radio deliver to Western homes.
The other used to be hard pressed to hear the broadcasts of the BBC
or Voice of America. In Moscow Solzhenitsyn saw in Sartre, who was
a guest of the Writers' Union, the accomplice of his persecutors. When
Solzhenitsyn reached Switzerland it may well be that he became, in
Sartre's eyes, an ally of the hated enemy. Beyond their mutual non-
comprehension we can discern two quite alien worlds, the world of
the Russian dissident and the world of the "European Leftist."

A Western writer who is officially received by an authoritarian or
totalitarian regime finds himself in an awkward position—a fact of
which he cannot but be aware if he has the slightest intelligence and
capacity for self-criticism. I for my part have never been disconcerted
by this. In Moscow I took part in a congress organized by UNESCO
where in the course of the sessions, and to the considerable delight of
the younger Soviet delegates, I several times clashed with an old
Stalinist, the Vice-President of the Academy of Sciences. In Spain I
consistently refused to lecture whenever my hosts demanded to see a
synopsis of my speech in advance. Incidentally, in my conversations
with Spanish intellectuals and with bank officials too I more than once
ran up against the Marxist "Vulgate." The higher the positions which
these dissidents occupied in the present system, the more radical their
views tended to be. In Mexico my main discussions were with intellectuals sympathetic to Fidel Castro but who conformed to the regime
in their country. When I went to Brazil, President Goulart had not yet
been overthrown by the military. It was in my journalistic capacity
that I traveled to Cuba: I was not received by Fidel Castro, but had a
long talk with Rafael Carlos Rodriguez, Head of the Cuban Commu-

nist Party, who explained to me in Marxist Spanish how a proletarian revolution could have been brought about by members of the petty bourgeoisie.

Sartre and Simone de Beauvoir enjoyed privileges of quite a different order. Their fame has allowed them to pass the frontiers even of countries ruled by rightist military regimes. In Cuba they were able to approach that historic hero who was to remain friendly towards Sartre as long as he sang the praises of Castroism and remained ignorant of the fate of the dissidents (already present in their thousands in Cuban prisons at the time he made friends with Castro). The day that Sartre signed a document in support of an imprisoned Cuban writer (who, incidentally, was set free after acknowledging the error of his way, if my memory serves me well), the Supremo thundered out against these petty bourgeois and their scrupulous consciences. The Sartres lost interest in Cuba and the Cubans.

The Sartres really do have something of a gay-Parisian background: they are littérateurs first and foremost and for them their works are just as important as people are. Sometimes they bring off the difficult trick—he despite his genius, she despite her education and intelligence—of seeming simple-minded. How can Simone de Beauvoir possibly fail to understand Solzhenitsyn's rebuff? How can she possibly fail to envisage the anger or hilarity with which Soviet dissidents greet a statement such as the following, from *The Critique of Dialectical Reason*: "Marxism is the unsurpassable philosophy of our era"? A statement, by the way, which one could not but describe as plain stupid if it stemmed from the pen of a lesser figure than Jean-Paul Sartre. A more temperate Western author might perhaps have said that Marxism remains at the center of philosophical inquiry, while Solzhenitsyn calmly writes that "Marxism has fallen so low that it can now arouse only contempt. No one in our country who wishes to be taken seriously, not even a schoolboy, can talk about Marxism today without a smile."

Marxism (and Solzhenitsyn is not interested in distinguishing between Marxism and Marxism-Leninism, between ordinary Marxism and subtle Marxism) is quite simply the doctrine in whose name the Bolsheviks seized power, destroyed first political parties, then the peasantry, set up concentration camps and murdered millions upon millions of ordinary citizens. More than this: in Solzhenitsyn's eyes Marxism as an ideology is the root of all ill, the source of falsehood, the principle of evil:

Fortunately, it is in the nature of the human being to seek a *justification* for his actions.

Macbeth's self-justifications were feeble—and his conscience devoured him. Yes even Iago was a little lamb too. The imagination and spiritual strength of Shakespeare's evildoers stopped short at a dozen corpses. Because they had no *ideology*.

Ideology—that is what gives evildoing its long-sought justification and gives the evildoer the necessary steadfastness and determination. That is the social theory which helps to make his acts seem good instead of bad in his own and others' eyes, so that he won't hear reproaches and curses, but will receive praise and honors. That was how the agents of the Inquisition fortified their wills: by invoking Christianity; the conquerors of foreign lands, by extolling the grandeur of their Motherland; the colonizers, by civilization; the Nazis, by race; the Jacobins (early and late), by equality, brotherhood, and the happiness of future generations.

Thanks to *ideology* the twentieth century was fated to experience evildoing on a scale calculated in the millions.[2]

I have chosen this passage from *The Gulag Archipelago* for two reasons. Firstly because it goes to the very heart of the question, to the ideology which alone can give the criminal a clear conscience. In addition it mentions other doctrines besides Marxism—those of Hitler, of the colonists, of the nationalists. Nor does Solzhenitsyn, a Christian himself, forget that Christianity can serve to bolster up the inquisitors. He tends to afford Marxists, if not Marxism itself, a special place, rather as if the quantitative difference brought with it a corresponding modification in quality (he will, I trust, forgive this reference to one of the laws of Engels' and Hegel's dialectic). During the eighty years preceding the Revolution of 1917 there were seventeen executions a year. When the Spanish Inquisition was in full swing the figure was ten per month. In the first years of Bolshevik rule it ran at one thousand a month. At the height of Stalin's Terror the monthly total of executions reached forty thousand. Evil needs an ideology before it can operate in millions. And this need is all the more urgent if the Terror is to remain unrecognized or even acclaimed. But the Sartres, more than other Western writers, justify Evil by justifying the justification of it. They are not Marxists—they have no wish to give up any of *their* freedom but by philosophical means they justify other men's deprivation of liberty at the hands of totalitarianism and Terror. Sartre is the philosopher of ideological thinking.

I do not wish to trace Sartre's political and philosophical career, beginning with *Nausea* in which he makes of the humanist a figure of fun, through to his dialogues with Left extremists. Favorably disposed towards the Munich agreement before 1938 because of his pacifism, after the liberation he adopted positions which can be reconciled only with the greatest difficulty. Among this long series of attitudes, however, certain postulates and maxims are to be found which one would be inclined to ascribe to a somewhat degenerate practical sense. The most important ones are: that anti-communists are blackguards; that the only people who have the right to criticize communism are those who become involved in the movement; that it is impossible not to be a Marxist since Marxism sets its indelible stamp upon our age. These postulates have consequences which Sartre has strictly observed. At a time when people in the West were discussing the fact that there were concentration camps in the Soviet Union, he directed his anger not so much against the Soviet authorities who had established these camps, nor against the communists who had denied their existence, but against the anti-communists and the so-called Rightists who were suspected of rejoicing in the fact.

At no time did the philosopher of peace stand closer to the communists than in the period of the peace movement, in other words in the Stalin era. Indefatigable defender of the persecuted, so long as their hangmen did not appeal to Marx or other acceptable doctrines, actively, passionately interceding for the release of Henry Martin (does anyone still remember that sailor?), or against the execution of the Rosenbergs, he belonged to the front organizations along with communists and fellow-travelers, and without any perceptible conflict with his conscience. In a word, he provides the perfect example of that Western "Leftism" which Solzhenitsyn repeatedly pillories in his book. "Leftism" is, so to speak, the elaboration of the principle according to which everything is measured by two different scales. It matters little what a man of the Right actually says, his views will be rejected in advance. If he mentions Soviet concentration camps, then it is not because he loves freedom and loathes the repression of one man by his fellows, but because for reasons which he cannot admit he has chosen the camp of the "Rightists" (or the conservatives, or the reactionaries); he is looking for reasons which he *can* own to for a choice to which he cannot own. A Rightist, authoritarian or moderate regime without any concentration camps must be condemned by the same token, and more fiercely than a Soviet regime which bears the responsibility for tens of millions of deaths within the space of sixty years.

Nor does it help to appeal to those texts in which Sartre at long last comes to grips with Stalinism. After the suppression of the Hungarian revolution he wrote *The Ghost of Stalin*, but without expressing the slightest regret for his former views and activities. Nor did he question the fundamentals of "Leftism," for this bloody monster was once again none other than Socialism. In other words he disavowed neither his "Leftism" nor his affiliation with the communists. Nor did he come any nearer to doing so in his *Socialism That Came In from the Cold*: in between the lines he foisted the blame for "inhuman socialism" upon the Russian influence, upon fortuitous factors. The Czechs' humane socialism lay in the camp of the Left and of Marxism. The ideology was intact.

The Critique of Dialectical Reason lends itself both to a Marxist-Leninist and a Leftist (*gauchiste*) interpretation. According to Maurice Merleau-Ponty ultra-Bolshevism expresses itself in a breakdown, in a revolt, in action, but doubts remain. Is it really the Party which with its merciless discipline (*fraternité-terreur*) takes it upon itself to wrench men locked in "practico-inertia" out of this state? Or is it rather the spontaneity of the group symbolized by the masses in the exalted days of Revolution, the fusion of the individual's consciousness with that of the others, which furnishes the model for the future society, for the truly liberated consciousness, transparent to all? Whatever the answer may turn out to be, Leftism remains, remains intact and, one may say, is still gaining in intensity. Ultra-Bolshevism demands revolt or, to put it more clearly, the categorical imperative of violence.

After 1968 Sartre discovered that ultimately his philosophy was more likely to culminate in anarchy than in Sovietism. But why hesitate between the one and the other? Why justify that total power, that cruelest of powers in our century, the power which enables us to do anything at all out of revulsion at the power of the state? Marxism itself explains nothing.

Much as Sartre may have busied himself with the writings of Marx, there is barely a trace of this reading to be found. Sartre alludes to the first volume of *Capital* and the theory of surplus value, but this is grist to his mill since it seems to show that the entrepreneur exploits the employee and the capitalist the wage-earner. There are no grounds for suspecting that he is even remotely interested in the relations between Ricardo and Marx or in Marx's place in the history of political economy. As for the unsurpassable philosophy of our epoch, which has incidentally been essentially sterile for more than half a century now, Sartre summarizes it in vague, indeed almost meaningless phrases, such as, Men make their own history but on the basis of the given material conditions. Putting it differently: it was not Marxism which brought this by nature anarchistic man to the point of sympathizing with Stalin's Terror, but, on the contrary, his inclination towards anarchy induced him to accept Marxism, which remains alien to him or of which he retains only the negations and the utopia.

What has produced the vacillation between the two extremes of anarchy and totalitarianism, what has made of Sartre a philosopher of ideology instead of a mere ideologist, is the cult of violence turned moralism, the sternness of a Protestant moralism swung round into rejection of the social order. But what is staggering is that on this long path Sartre expresses a moral condemnation of those who think differently from himself. Who accords him the right to mount the throne of Jupiter or Jehovah, to sound the hearts of men?

How, one may ask, are we to know since after all there is no possibility of distinguishing between Good and Evil, between good and evil conduct, except within history, and since after all we must wait for a social order free from exploitation and repression before we can begin to write our ethics? It is enough to call for the categorical imperative of Revolt (or even the categorical imperative of violence) and the game is won. How quickly it goes! A few thousand students occupy the Sorbonne, rebuild the University and the world from scratch, sleep with one another and talk, talk, talk. . . .

Since neither Sartre's Marxism nor his Existentialism has a clearly delineated political content, he can pass from the *Rassemblement démocratique révolutionnaire* to fraternizing with Stalinism, can admit that there are millions of labor-camp prisoners in the Soviet Union without this causing him to break with the communists, he can condemn the suppression of the Hungarian revolution as if it were separate from the whole of that which he approves of or puts up with. He can write that the dictatorship of the proletariat is a contradictory concept while simultaneously describing himself as a Marxist, and that without his conscience experiencing the slightest trouble; and finally he can distance himself from the communists because a few thousand students or workers have had the experience of his *groupe en fusion* and have dreamed of his anarchy. He can even muster a degree of sympathy for the left-wing extremists of the Baader-Meinhof gang, and he who loses no sleep over millions of concentration camp inmates, holds press-conferences to expose the misery and loneliness to which Baader and his companions are condemned (he probably does not know that Ulrike Meinhof originally received money from the East German Secret Service).

The fact that he has pilgrimaged in undiscriminating succession to Belgrade, Havana, Moscow or Peking bothers him not at all; evidently, he feels responsible for all men, but not for his previous conduct. It may be that he feels more at ease in the company of Victor[3] than of Stalin (whom he has probably never seen) or even Fidel Castro (in whom he believed he had found a friend). Nevertheless, he has not dissociated himself from his earlier positions. Here is the Right and here the Left. Here are the concentration camps which one does not accept and here the ones which one does. There are good murderers and evil ones. Marxism remains the unsurpassable philosophy of our epoch, and those who base themselves upon it are always on the right side, while those who defend freedom against the advocates of that philosophy are in the wrong.

In a certain sense Simone de Beauvoir is right in saying that Alexander Solzhenitsyn does not know Sartre well (although he knows him better than Sartre knows Solzhenitsyn). And yet she is wrong about the main point: if the *zek* had known the "ruler of minds" better, he would have still seen no sense in talking to him. As a personality Sartre embodies everything which Solzhenitsyn loathes: the rejection of moral guidelines, the refusal to accept the age-old distinction between good and evil, the sacrifice of men's lives and the justification of crimes by appeals to an indefinite future ("indefinite" in all its senses), in short, the evil of ideology—a kind of evil which in Sartre's case takes on a pure form—indirect, delegated evil. He kills nobody; he would not hurt a fly and his only participation in history is through his pen. Now he gives Stalin his half-hearted applause, now Castro his unreserved though short-lived, greeting, but never does he condemn the practice which Solzhenitsyn finds detestable: the practice of committing crimes in the name of ideology. "Ruler of minds" in the West, Solzhenitsyn writes. Although even in his own lifetime Sartre's only place is in the past, he is still, if not the "ruler," then at least the most representative figure (if only in caricature) of the European intelligentsia, or of the intellectual Left, whichever description is preferable. It matters little that nowadays few of them still read *Being and Nothingness* or *The Critique of Dialectical Reason*, or that Foucault, Deleuze or Althusser have supplanted him; he is the one who more than any other has made "Leftism" respectable, indeed obligatory. To a Solzhenitsyn and to other Soviet dissidents none of the Rightist authoritarian regimes, neither the Greek military junta nor Franco in Spain, seemed comparable with the tyranny which weighs upon the peoples of the Soviet Union. Not one of them has perpetrated so many crimes; not one has so enslaved free thought. But the Sartres and all their disciples forbid us to condemn the Soviet Union unless we first embrace Leftism and join the Socialist movement.

What would have come of a dialogue between Solzhenitsyn and Sartre? Nothing. Each of them would have rejected any comparison of respective number of victims under one form of despotism or another, albeit for quite different reasons: Sartre—because under certain kinds of despotism men were ostensibly liberated, whereas under others hereditary injustice and disorder were upheld; Solzhenitsyn—because, over and above the number of victims, the Soviet regime seems of its very nature perverse, for it lies and compels others to lie. The Greek Colonels "saved" Greece; Franco "saved" Christian Spain; neither of them created a world of mandatory falsehood. In Spain censorship was called censorship, not "the leading role of the Party." In the universities and in the streets everyone could speak his own language; all books, or nearly all, could be translated and published. The regime, born in a brutal revolution, remained brutal till the end; it was neither democratic, nor liberal; but it was not totalitarian, and crimes there were not sanctified by ideology.

Compared with Stalin's regime, that of Franco may justly have been regarded as liberal. A pious man of the Left holds such a view to be scandalous and monstrous. Solzhenitsyn holds it to be true and evident. It takes the whole "Leftism" of the Western intelligentsia to doubt it.

My friend Manès Sperber joined the Communist Party in Vienna after the first world war. Had I, like him, witnessed the collapse of a world, I might perhaps have succumbed to the same temptation. But never since the day in the mid-thirties when I first met him in André Malraux's home have I seen his disillusionment cloud the sobriety of his judgment. We have not always agreed in our assessment of this or that event; no one can claim the truth for his own. If the past can of its very nature be subjected to legitimate reinterpretation, how then can history as it evolves and shapes itself in the present lend itself to unerring diagnosis?

Our friendship has survived forty years without a setback; this is due not only to the fact that he broke with a revolution betrayed, with a totalitarian regime, with an ideology which henceforth served to justify the unjustifiable, but also to the fact that his view of the Marxist tragedy coincided both with my own instinctive liberalism and with the faith of the Soviet dissidents.

Solzhenitsyn's message can be summarized, it seems to me, in two fundamental sentences: There is something worse than poverty and repression—and that something is the Lie; the lesson this century teaches us is to recognize the deadly snare of ideology, the illusion that men and social organizations can be transformed at a stroke.

Solzhenitsyn does not call for a crusade against Soviet totalitarianism; he does not wish upon his country a revolution which could cause chaos and bring bloodshed. The writer, his country's greatest and perhaps the greatest of our time, takes, and will continue to take, offense at the conspiracy of unrepentant ideologues which more than ever dominates the press, radio and television of the West. But he will gather about him in a vast silent mass all those who see no other defense against the raging of fanaticism and who have no other hope for the future than in respect for moral laws and the rejection of ideological knavery. He had nothing to say to Sartre and his like; in Manès Sperber he encountered a brother.

Notes

1. Alexander Solzhenitsyn, *The Oak and the Calf* (New York: Harper and Row, 1979), p. 119.
2. Alexander Solzhenitsyn, *The Gulag Archipelago*, I–II (New York: Harper and Row, 1974), p. 173–74.
3. A left-wing worker.

Part Four

Aron and the Philosophy of History

Introduction

History as Usual or the End of History?

Aron's political thought is defined by a paradoxical but instructive stance toward history; Aron paid very real and detailed attention to the concrete circumstances and contingencies of "history in the making," but he categorically refused an "idolatry of history": the belief in the illusion that a historical process would put an end to the dialectic of necessities, choices, and accidents that defines the human adventure. Aron was simultaneously a philosopher who made "politics and history" the stuff of his reflection and an incisive opponent of all "idolatrous" historicisms.

An impressive application of Aron's philosophy of history to the interpretation of the character of the twentieth century can be found in his 1960 essay, "The Dawn of Universal History." In *The Liberal Political Science of Raymond Aron: A Critical Introduction* (Rowman & Littlefield, 1992), I devote two chapters to a commentary on this study. I argue that "The Dawn of Universal History" contains and illustrates the key elements of Aron's "political science" and "philosophy of history." I refer readers interested in pursuing the deeper recesses of Aron's thought to that more comprehensive analysis.

This text conveys Aron's rejection of global historical determinism and his theoretical defense of free but limited and constrained human action. It is an effort to analyze change and continuity within modernity while avoiding both pessimistic (e.g., Martin Heidegger and Oswald Spengler) and optimistic (e.g., Auguste Comte and Karl Marx) accounts of political and historical evolution. However, Aron's political science is not merely a return to an older tradition of political reflection. Aron understood the distinctively "modern" (i.e., progress, science, industry, the sense of historical consciousness) in terms of its dialectical interaction and interpenetration with permanent human and political phenomena. At its deepest level, Aron's work embodies a

127

dialectical reflection on the relationship between the permanent features of human and social nature and the necessities and contingencies of historical evolution in modern times.

"The Dawn of Universal History" lucidly outlines the political history of the modern world from the guns of August 1914 through the middle years of the Cold War. Written in 1960, "The Dawn of Universal History" no longer adequately describes the present "diplomatic–strategic constellation" as Aron called the international tableau of regimes, resources, ideas, and military forces. The great schism, the civil war between "industrial societies" of the East and West, is at an end. The victory of the Western democracies in the Cold War and the nearly unchallenged "theoretical" ascendancy of liberal, democratic, and capitalist "values" in the "developed" world has led some, most notably Francis Fukuyama in his international best-seller *The End of History and the Last Man* (Free Press, 1992), to assert that, in principle, history has come to an end.

Moreover, according to this view, atavistic political and social impulses and passions, such as xenophobic nationalism will continue to plague the former communist bloc, where rational modernity has been stymied by oligarchic despotisms justified in the name of a decayed, pseudo-rationalist ideology. But these are best viewed as the rearguard actions of peoples who are experiencing the infantile traumas accompanying the return to "normal" social and political life. And, of course, the peoples in the so-called underdeveloped nations remain immersed in ethnic, national, and religious strife. They are decidedly "historical" in their sentiments, beliefs, and behaviors. But even they are tempted by the West's technological dynamism, the allure of the "VCR," and by its discourse of human rights and equality. Despite abundant *empirical* evidence to the contrary, Fukuyama sees no credible or widely accepted challenge to liberal democracy remaining in the world. There remain only more or less vigorous atavisms or anachronisms vainly resisting the unfolding of history's purposes.

The anti-communist Fukuyama gives a historicist and optimistic account, one is almost tempted to say a Marxist account, of the collapse of communist "modernity" and of the future of liberal democracy and the liberal idea. In principle, democratic polities with "mixed" capitalist economies, in a variety of permutations from the American to the Scandinavian, are the only genuinely legitimate political orders today. According to this view, the liberal democratic regimes are "rational" regimes because they embody the principle of "mutual recognition"—the principle of the dignity of all which is to be reflected in the reality of universal citizenship.[1]

Like Fukuyama, Aron believed that one could speak intelligently about "universal history." He did not dismiss the speculations of philosophers of history as "literary" or unscientific in character. He wished to do justice to both mankind's increasing consciousness of belonging to *one* drama, *one* adventure and the enduring sources of its divisions and disunities. But the "dawn of universal history" was not coextensive with the "end of history" for Aron.

It is fair to say on the basis of his lifelong reflection on the philosophy of history and the nature of modern politics that Aron would not amend his repeatedly stated objection to the notion of the "end of history." He had too great a sense of historical tragedy, too much of a classical or premodern recognition of the human capacity for evil and the inherent imperfections of human nature, and too strong an appreciation of the instability and unpredictability of social passions, to believe that liberal democracy or any other "rational" regime could ever become the universal and permanent political norm. This was for him a "hope based only on faith." In addition, he was aware of what he called the "disillusions of progress," of the fact that the "contradictions" of modern societies inevitably engender novel alienations and discontents, discontents that simultaneously resuscitate atavistic social yearnings and feed into utopian hopes for a society without conflicts or contradictions.

The political defeat of Left and Right totalitarianisms will not eliminate the "contradictions" inherent in dynamic, mass democratic societies. Nor will it, in all likelihood, lead to the establishment of a "new world order" characterized by the unchallenged hegemony of the liberal, commercial regimes of the West. *History as usual*, with its conflicts within and between nations and regimes, relentlessly unfolds. Aron's work, therefore, continues to raise compelling doubts about the wisdom of dismissing "dramatic" history as a residue of a past that we moderns have irrevocably left behind.

"The Dawn of Universal History" was first published in English translation in 1961. The following is a new, somewhat more literal translation, prepared specifically for this volume. The third section of the essay has been edited to exclude somewhat dated reflections and speculations on the nature of the international situation in 1960 and the future of East-West relations. Ellipses have been included to allow readers to know where excisions have been made.

Notes

1. Fukuyama's optimism is modified in the last part of his book by the specter of Nietzsche's "last man." Fukuyama fears that the universal triumph of liberal democratic "rationality" may threaten that human seriousness which depends upon the cultivation and exercise of human spiritedness. Fukuyama fears the enervation of the human soul in a world bereft of great projects and enterprises.

The Dawn of Universal History

Raymond Aron

1961

I believe a few words are required to justify the title of this lecture and to dispel the false impression it could not fail to make. A publisher present at this occasion is responsible, both for my presence here and for the subject I am going to sketch more than treat.

A year or two ago, this publisher—who is publishing a series of books devoted to the epochs of civilization—asked me if I would agree to write a history of the world since 1914. I immediately responded that no serious historian would agree to undertake such a task. We have lived a part of history since 1914, each of us at his place, with his passions or his prejudices, but no one among us has lived the entirety, none is the master of an enormous, dispersed matter, no one has yet raised to the level of consciousness these events swollen with human pain, with unprecedented crimes, with unlimited promises.

Then, after some reflection, I added: no serious historian would have the pretense you suggest to me, but I am not a historian. Perhaps as philosopher or sociologist, it would not be impossible for me to write an essay which would uncover some of the original traits of our age and which, in particular, would emphasize what I call the dawn of universal history. For the first time the so-called advanced societies are in the process of living one and the same history. For the first time, perhaps, one can speak of "human society." The lecture which follows contains some of the ideas which will figure in the introduction and conclusion of the book I have committed myself to write.

I am not unaware that such an essay runs the risk of being judged severely by many of my colleagues, whether they be philosophers or historians. Sociology has not yet obtained citizenship in traditional English universities or, at least, it dissembles itself under less Americanized words (such as anthropology). As for the philosophy of history, whether it identifies with Bossuet or Hegel, with Marx or Toynbee, it is held to be at best a literary rather than scientific endeavor to which writers, but not respectable thinkers, can devote themselves.

What can I say in my defense? First of all, I am more aware than anyone else of the precariousness, of the vulnerability of the essay I intend to write. I make this clear from the beginning: this essay is neither a matter of a narrative such as that of Thucydides (there are too many events and they are too incoherent), nor of a synthesis like that of Jacob Burckhardt's work on the Italian renaissance. It will be an essay which presents itself as such, limited in its perspective by the inevitable limitations of the author's personality, marked by the experience and the aspirations of a man engaged in a country, a generation, and an intellectual system.

Why would anyone reproach me for writing such an essay, stripped of all ambition, since (consciously or not) we are all writing it? Perhaps the scholar is capable of regarding past centuries with the gaze of the pure spectator; perhaps the historian of Athens and Sparta, of Rome and Carthage, of the Pope and the Emperor, of the Holy Roman Empire and the French monarchy, no longer shows the passions which moved the agents, perhaps he is able to comprehend with the same serenity the combatants of all the camps, the beliefs they had in common, the interests which opposed them to each other, and the catastrophes or the accomplishments of which, together, unwittingly, they were the artisans. But when we open the morning newspapers, when we vote for some candidate, we are not hesitating to situate ourselves in our age and situate our age in time. Whoever endeavors to raise to consciousness the fate—lived through or experienced by the Frenchman or Englishman of the 20th century—gives himself "an interpretation of the world since 1914." I will attempt to render this interpretation of the 20th century less fragmentary and less inspired by passion. Here is the route that I will take.

Part I

Since the beginning of the 19th century, all the generations in Europe have had the feeling of living in an unprecedented epoch. Was this a conviction whose constancy demonstrated that each time it was without foundation? Was it a sort of premonition whose falsehood for those who came before us and whose truth for us were confirmed by our experience? Finally, if we hesitate to dismiss all the generations, or all except our own, is not there another hypothesis, namely that they all were right, but all collectively rather than each one for itself, and that they all were right, but differently than they thought?

In other words, it appears to me true or at least plausible that during the course of the past century, humanity has lived through a sort of revolution—perhaps it would be better called a mutation—whose initial phases are anterior to the 20th century and whose pace has accelerated during the past decades. This historical mutation each generation and each thinker has attempted to define since the beginning of the past century. Saint-Simon and Auguste Comte called it industrial society; Alexis de Tocqueville, democratic society; Karl Marx, capitalist society. Let us return to the great doctrinaires of the first half of the past century: our ideologies, if not our ideas, derive from their works. By confronting their diagnoses and their prophecies with what has occurred between their time and ours we will give an initial definition of what I have just called a historical mutation.

Let us begin with the school of Saint-Simon and Auguste Comte, which is returning to fashion for an immediately intelligible reason: the building up of large industry, in some respects analogous, on both sides of the Iron Curtain has finally obliged observers to recognize that there was a type of society of which the Soviet regimes and Western regimes represented two species or two versions. Why not call this type of society "industrial society," since its main point is the development of industry?

Such, in fact, was the central intention of Saint-Simon and Auguste Comte. Both saw a new society forming before their eyes, which they called industrial society and of which Europe was the creator. Better than Saint-Simon and even Saint-Simonism, Auguste Comte stated precisely the essential traits of this new society. Although the founder of positivism is rarely read today and even more rarely studied seriously, the formulation he gave of industrial society will provide our point of departure.

Like Saint-Simon, Comte opposes industrial, agricultural, and financial producers to the political or military elites which, in a society devoted to peaceful labor, represent a survival from a feudal and theological past. Like all human society, industrial society has a primary objective and this latter is henceforth the exploitation of natural resources. The time of wars and conquests, of Caesars, is past. Despite his genius, Napoleon was guilty of a serious crime in the eyes of the philosophers of history, that of *anachronism*. The Roman conquests had meaning and fecundity because they prepared the unified world in which Christianity was to spread, and because the collectivities devoted to war were one day to arrive at peace though the victory of the strongest. In our epoch, conquests are unjustifiable because they no longer serve any purpose, and because peoples have shown, by their spontaneous resistance and final triumph, the error of he who, harvesting the legacy of the Revolution, transformed into hatred the sympathy the people of Europe had for the enterprise which the French people by themselves had inaugurated for the profit of all.

Reasoning with a dogmatism which some will see as the tendency of sociologists as such, Auguste Comte draws the consequences, all the consequences, of this change of objective. It is work, not war, which henceforth represents the supreme value. It is work which creates the elites, the directors of modern society; it is from work that each derives the prestige public opinion bestows; it is work which gives to each the place he occupies in the social hierarchy. Moreover, work is, and ought to be free: families are no longer simply rooted in a class or an occupation; mobility becomes the rule across generations. Individuals can now aspire to a status proportionate to their merit, without reference to the position that their parents occupied. In the order marked by wage earners, Comte perceives, not a modern form of slavery or servitude, but the promise of the liberation of men.

Europe, more precisely the nations of Western Europe—England, France, Italy, Spain, Germany—constitute for Comte the avant-garde of humanity. They were ahead of the other peoples, but in an ultimately common task: the exploitation of the planet, the actualization of industrial society, the unification of all the collectivities scattered throughout the five continents into a peaceful community. Moreover, according to the high priest of positivism, Europe's advance founded more obligations than privileges. Auguste Comte warned his contemporaries against the temptation of colonial conquests. A thousand times he denounced the occupation of Algeria and even expressed the hope that the Arabs "would vigorously expel" the French if the latter didn't have the intelligence and virtue to withdraw themselves.

It would be easy—and some have not restrained themselves—to wax ironic about Comte's prophecies. Insofar as he proclaimed that the times of European wars and colonial conquests were passed, he was roundly mistaken. But if one considers Comte not as a prophet but as a counsellor to princes and peoples, he was wiser than events were. He did not announce the future such as it became but such as it would have been if history had unfolded according to the wisdom of men of good will.

Comte believed that the industrial society in the process of spreading throughout Western Europe was and would continue to be exemplary for all humanity. He was right on this very point. He was wrong, of course, to restrict himself to a perspective concentrated on Europe, to fail to recognize the originality of other civilizations, to believe in

a rigorous dependence of forms of political organization and of beliefs *vis-à-vis* social types, and to dismiss the permanence of ways of
thinking he called theological and metaphysical. But, with respect to
the relations between work and war, between the exploitation of natural resources and the exploitation of man by man, he comprehended
with an incontestable clairvoyance the revolution which both governors and peoples today have painfully come to admit: wars between
industrial societies are simultaneously ruinous and sterile and non-in-
dustrialized societies, which we call underdeveloped, cannot but take
industrial societies as models. In this sense Europe was, rightly, exemplary. But Europe would be wrong, Comte said, to impose this
example, profiting from a temporary superiority in order to reopen the
age of great invasions. What good is it to kill, enslave, and pillage?
Gold and silver no longer are true riches. The only wealth is rationally organized work. Slavery was necessary in the distant past in order
to accustom men inclined to sloth and dissipation to regular activity.
But the formation of European man to the rationality of work has progressed sufficiently so that constraint is no longer useful. Wars, like
colonial conquests, are henceforth anachronistic.

Both continue to occur, but they appear today as irrational, at least
if one supposes, with Comte, that men do not make war for its own
sake or for the sole intoxication of conquering. If the major objective
of industrial societies is work in view of well-being—which is what
spokesmen for both Soviet and Western societies affirm—then the two
European wars of this century were useless and the third war of the
century ought not to take place.

Let us turn now to the other great doctrinaire belonging to the
generation after Comte's, namely, Karl Marx. He, too, discerned a
historical mutation, and even though he employed different concepts
and words, he placed the emphasis on the same major facts: the development of productive forces (the merit for which he attributed to
the bourgeoisie) had been more rapid than in any previous century. In
a few decades, the conquering bourgeoisie had overturned the conditions and techniques of work in common more than the elites of feudal or military societies had done over the span of a thousand years.

The high priest of socialism agrees with the high priest of positivism in highlighting the heterogeneous natures of traditional societies
and modern society. Both saw the originality of the latter in the primacy of work, of science applied to the technique of production, and
in the augmentation of collective resources which results. The major
difference between the two doctrines is that Marx believes that the
conflict between employers and employees is fundamental, while

Comte takes this conflict as secondary, a symptom of a social disintegration which progress in organization will correct.

Marx has a tendency to explain everything—misery in the midst
of abundance and despite the growth in productive forces, the alienation of workers, the despotism of the property-owning minority—by
the conflict between employers and employees, by the class struggle
between capitalists and proletarians. He also has an apocalyptic vision of the future of capitalism—the continued aggravation of the
fundamental conflict between the capitalists and proletariats results in
the final explosion. In the same stroke he sketches an idyllic portrait
of the post-capitalist regime, which he never describes but whose benefits he evokes in contrast. If social inequities, the exploitation of man
by man, class struggle, and worker alienation are due to the specific
traits of capitalism such as private ownership of the instruments of
production, and the ownership by the capitalist minority of economic
power and, by intermediaries, of political power—then, the elimination of private property and the proletarian revolution will put an end
to the prehistory of humanity and will open an era when social
progress will no longer require political revolutions.

It seems to me that on this essential point where the two disagree,
Marx perhaps was correct in the short term, but wrong in the long
run. The conflicts between employers and employees within industries
or for the distribution of national income were not decisive. Generally, these conflicts burned more intensely during the initial phases of
industrialization than in industrial societies which have reached matu-
rity. Working classes organized in unions, protected by social legislation, often represented in parliament by powerful socialist parties,
continue to make demands, but they have been converted to peaceful
and legal methods. They do not wish for a revolution which would
introduce the dictatorship of the proletariat; they do not even know
clearly what a proletarian revolution would be. The proof is the fact
evident to them and to most observers: that private ownership of the
instruments of production, as it is practiced in today's Western societies, prohibits neither the development of productive forces nor the el-
evation of the standard of living of the masses. Whatever might be
the judgment one makes on the relative productivity of the Soviet and
Western regimes, it is clear that the former does not mean abundance
and the latter misery. The differences between the two regimes are
much more striking in society than in industry, in the structure of the
state and public powers than in those of society. Industrial society, as
Comte affirmed, does entail a technico-bureaucratic hierarchy, in which
free workers are integrated.

The conflicts which dominated the 20th century and determined its course were national or imperial more than social. Even as doctrinaires August Comte and Karl Marx did not mistake the historical mutation taking place before their eyes, but they did underestimate the persistence of the traditional aspect of history: the rise and fall of empires, the rivalry of regimes, the disastrous and beneficial exploits of great men.

In different ways, both underestimated the properly political element. Marx wrote as if the political regime of capitalism was adequately defined by the power of the bourgeoisie, as if the political regime of socialism was defined adequately by the semi-mythological formula of the dictatorship of the proletariat. Auguste Comte on the other hand left power to the administrators of work in common, occupied solely with lessening its rigors and forestalling its excesses by means of the resistance of public opinion, that of women or of workers. Both ignore the alternative erected by Alexis de Tocqueville: yes, modern societies will be commercial and industrial societies, with egalitarian tendencies and characterized by increased mobility, for thus the profound tendencies of modern societies will have it. But modern societies still retain the choice between, on one hand, the despotism of one, ruling over millions of individuals whose differences are effaced in a uniformity of condition and servitude, and, on the other, the liberty of all, perhaps similar in comfort and a sort of mediocrity, but preserving their rights of initiative, judgment, and faith.

Misunderstanding the partial autonomy of the political order, the doctrinaires of sociology reasoned as if history, in the sense of the succession of wars and empires, of victories and defeats, was henceforth finished. Today, in 1960, the century we have lived in and through appears double or dual to me. It is shot through by an intellectual, technical, and economic revolution which, like a cosmic force, draws humanity towards an unknown future, but which, in certain regards, resembles many precedents, it is not the first century of great wars. On one hand, the necessity of progress; on the other, *history as usual* and the drama of empires, armies, and heroes.

The fundamental movement appears clearly in the statistics concerning intellectual and industrial production. At the beginning of the century men annually consumed a few tons of oil; today they consume almost a thousand million, yes, a thousand million tons. And the increase continues to the rhythm of 10 percent or more per year. A few million tons of steel fifty years ago represented the annual production of a great power; today it represents the annual increase in production of a great power. Robert Oppenheimer indicated a figure to me which profoundly struck me. Of all the scientists who have existed since there were men capable of thought, 90 percent are living today. The acceleration of history is inscribed in these statistics which illustrate the growing, and ever-faster growing, accumulation of knowledge and power, to use the terms of Auguste Comte.

Let us turn now towards traditional history. At each moment the mind is confounded: The event was and it could have not been, and how close it came to being other than it was! If the Germans had not sent two armies to the eastern front the night before the battle, would the miracle of the Marne have occurred? If the world crisis had not been prolonged for years, or if the French and English had reacted militarily to the return of German troops to the Rhineland, would the last world war have taken place? Without Churchill, would England have stood firm all alone against the Third Reich? If Hitler had not attacked Russia in 1941, what course would the greatest of wars have taken? Traditional history is action, that is to say it is made of decisions taken by men in a precise place and time. These decisions could have been different with another man in the same situation, or with the same man with another disposition. Now, no one can fix, either beforehand or retrospectively, the limits of the consequences that some of these localized and dated decisions generate.

In traditional history, accident seems to reign and grandeur is mixed with cruelty. The blood of innocents flows everywhere and the victories of princes are paid with the sacrifices of peoples. In the development of knowledge and power the law of necessity seems to reign and triumphant quantity ridicules the exploits of individuals or of the few. From time to time I dream about the incomparable history that Thucydides would write about the Thirty Years' War—1914–1945—whose first episode was compared by Thibaudet and Toynbee to the Peloponnesian War (but did they know in 1918 the peace of Versailles was only the truce of Nicias?). It probably would be necessary to complete the dramatic narrative by asking Marx or Colin Clark to write, not a narrative, but an analysis of the irresistible process of the industrialization of the planet. In a sense, this process is not less dramatic than the rise and fall of the Third Reich. Like a torrent, it carries everything in its current, it uproots age-old customs, it gives rise to factories and sprawling cities, it covers the entire planet with roads and railways, and offers to the masses the prospect of an abundance to which privileged nations bear witness and whose possibility they confirm, but it begins by wrenching men from the protection of beliefs and practices transmitted by the centuries and it delivers millions, without faith and law, to the uncertainties of an incomprehensible system commanded by mysterious machines.

I do not know if it will be possible for me, in the not yet written book, to convey to the reader the double sentiment of human action and necessity, of drama and process, of *history as usual* and the originality of industrial society. In this brief lecture allow me, after having underlined the differences between these two aspects of the century, to show how, in many ways, accident and necessity, drama and process, combined to weave the fabric of real history as it actually happened. Let us endeavor to draw out the law of industrial necessity at work in the drama of war and empires, the action of some giving form and shape to the process of industrialization. Then it will be appropriate, after this dual dialectical reversal, to ask if tomorrow process will be able to continue without drama.

Part II

There are, it seems to me, three non-exclusive ways to order in a necessary connection the succession of event-accidents, to underline the law of industrial progress within the drama of the great wars. The historian can explain by means of the industrial system either the origin of wars, their course, or their result. I do not believe in the first but I attribute much to the second and the third.

The first way, that of Lenin and the Marxists, sees in the drama only a spectacular episode of the process: the war of 1914 is not the expression of the traditional nature of human history; it is the fatal consequence of capitalism's contradictions, of the rivalries between capitalist states. This is not the place to analyze in detail a theory I have discussed a thousand times. But, in order that this exposition not be too incomplete, allow me to summarize in three propositions this classical thesis which still has more partisans than it merits.

1. Colonial imperialism is merely the extreme form of capitalist expansion across that world today which is called underdeveloped, across continents with traditional economies, whose weakness exposed them without defense to the rapacity of the great companies, to domination by the European states. 2. The peaceful division of the world into spheres of influence or into colonial empires was impossible. An ineluctable necessity pushed capitalists and capitalisms into the feverish quest for profits, for markets for their products, for human labor to exploit, for natural resources to develop. It was no more possible for capitalist economies to conclude a durable agreement concerning the division of the planet than it is possible within each country for individual capitalists to come to a mutual understanding concerning the sharing of the market or the cessation of competition. 3. The great war,[1] although fought on the old continent and apparently because of

properly European conflicts, really had for its cause and stakes the division of the planet. Without knowing it, French, Germans, and English died in order to enlarge the territory reserved for their countries in other parts of the world.

Now, to my mind these three propositions are not demonstrated and, in certain respects, they are refuted by the facts, or, at least, rendered improbable by an unprejudiced examination of the facts.

Under its different forms (the search for surplus profit by means of the development of rich natural resources or by the exploitation of human labor, the search for markets for manufactured products, the attempt to reserve to oneself privileges and to exclude competitors), economic expansion, even if it is supposed that it is tied to the essence of the capitalist regime, does not automatically entail colonialization and the assertion of political sovereignty. The latter does not appear useful or indispensable in the economic order except in order to exclude competitors, in order to guarantee for oneself advantages contrary to free competition. Now, the African territories which the Western European countries easily succeeded in conquering at the end of the 19th century and the beginning of the 20th, represented only a negligible fraction of the foreign commerce of the capitalist states; they absorbed only a small percentage of the capital that the old continent, banker of the world, placed outside. How is it possible then, in these conditions, to maintain the interpretation according to which colonial conquest was only the extreme form, the necessary expression, of an expansion inseparable from capitalist economies?

The second proposition also appears to me as arbitrary. We are well aware that within a country competitors often arrange to divide up markets for themselves and, thus, to suspend the free play (said to be inexorable) of the law of competition. *A fortiori*, how easy would have been the division of the world into spheres of influence, how facile the amiable regulating of African and Asiatic quarrels between European nations would have been, if they had had no other origin or stake than commercial interest! Precisely because of their industrial development, the European economies were each other's best clients. To the great capitalist enterprises, Western and Equatorial Africa, Algeria, and Morocco were only marginal zones of activity. German banks were less interested in Morocco than the Wilhelmstrasse wished. It was the chancelleries which rendered cooperation between German and French capitalists in Morocco impossible. The diplomats thought in terms of power, not because they were concerned for commercial interests or because the spokesmen for commercial interests pushed them to it, but because they had read their history and such had been the law of politics for millennia.

Finally, I am still waiting for someone to show me why a war, whose occasion was the German-Slavic rivalry in the Balkans, whose principal theater was Europe, whose stakes, in the minds of the agents, from the day when cannon thundered, were the power relations within the European diplomatic system, would have another origin and another meaning. By what subtlety can one arrive at showing that Africa and Asia were the cause while the gunshots which struck down the Archduke of Austria and the bombardment of Belgrade were the point of departure of the great war? How could faraway lands constitute more authentic stakes than the political status of central and eastern Europe?

In fact, to whoever interrogates the past without a preconceived opinion, all the facts orient the mind in the same direction, all suggest the same interpretation. The war of 1914–1918 was, at its origin, as consistent with traditional history as the preceding European wars and as the great war Thucydides narrated, which concerned all the cities composing the Hellenic system (as the states of the old continent composed the international system of Europe). A balanced system slides by itself towards an inexpiable war when it is rent into two coalitions, when one of the political units seems on the brink of establishing its hegemony over the entirety of the historical zone.

At the end of the 5th century B.C., Athens imperiled the liberties of the Greek cities. At the beginning of the 20th century, Germany represented the same peril to the nations of Europe. War to the death was not fatal, but it was fatal that, if war broke out, the other great powers immediately had the feeling of fighting for their existence and liberties. The immediate cause of the explosion—the status of Balkan Europe—was neither a simple occasion nor a pretext. Austria-Hungary and Turkey were multinational empires, one the legacy of times when the provinces belonged to sovereigns, the other of conquests with no other foundation or justification than the sword. But the eventual disintegration of these empires, especially that of Austria-Hungary, overturned the balance of power. Germany lost its principal ally: millions of Slavs might pass into the opposite camp. It is not unintelligible that the Reich would support the dual empire in an undertaking in which the latter looked for salvation and found death. It is no more unintelligible that from the beginning of August 1914, Great Britain and, especially, France would have feared a victory by Germany which for them would have meant the loss of their independence or, in any event, of their great-power status.

The war of 1914 began in the fashion of an ordinary war, but in the century of industry. It is in its development and its consequences that it bears the mark of the century to which it belongs and of which it is a tragic expression.

The great war of Thucydides was conducted from beginning to end with the same arms; and with the exception of some subtle combinations during the Sicilian expedition, it appears that the Greeks did not manifest during the course of innumerable battles as many technical or tactical inventions as they did deeds of heroism. The Thirty Years' War in the 20th century was opened by the gunshots of Sarajevo or by the Austrian cannon bombarding Belgrade, while it was closed with the atomic thunderclaps of Hiroshima and Nagasaki. Between 1914 and 1945, the technique of production and destruction had taken several steps.

Machine guns, light horse-drawn cannon, and heavy cannon are symbolic of the first battles. Continuous fronts, trenches, the accumulation and preparation of artillery, with ever more cannons and munitions, belong to the second stage, that of bloody but sterile combat during which tens of millions of men fell for a few kilometers of earth whose possession or loss meant nothing. Millions of airplanes, tanks, and trucks announced, during the last phase of hostilities, motorization and the collaboration of aviation and armored weapons which gave Hitler's Wehrmacht its spectacular triumphs from 1939 to 1941. The age of gasoline succeeded, without replacing the age of coal, light metals joined steel. But among the industrial countries qualitative superiority was, inevitably, precarious. The race for numerical superiority in men, arms, and munitions, which had been the dominant feature of the first war or the first phase of the Thirty Years' War, reappeared with greater *élan* during the second. With four thousand tanks and almost as many planes, Germany had defeated Poland, then France, piling up splendid victories during the summer of 1941. In 1944–45, the industrial machine of the anti-German coalition was running at full speed and the Soviet and Anglo-American armies were winning, thanks to a numerical superiority comparable to that of 1918.

The war had been one of industrial societies capable of mobilizing all their men and all their factories. Workers and soldiers, all citizens contributed to the collective effort. The *levée en masse* (mass conscription), called for by the decrees of the convention, actually took place. Success in organizing, including (the expression is Elie Halévy's) "the organization of enthusiasm" which, after the fact, survivors of the massacre reproached to the aged, was incomparable. This industrial war, conducted by civilians in uniform, was to animate the pacifist revolt which characterizes rather than contradicts bellicose epochs.

The second phase of the Thirty Years' War can be interpreted, like the first, with the aid of categories of traditional history: The defeated party, which for a long time had appeared the strongest, retained a sharp awareness, perhaps excessive but comprehensible, of the injustice of the conditions which had been imposed upon it and tried its luck a second time. There only would have been a true peace if all the rival states were satisfied. They were not, and so there were only truces. Any Germany would have been tempted to break the truce: the Germany of Hitler broke it cynically, with unlimited ambitions.

However, this traditional and partial interpretation is insufficient in many respects. Certainly, Jacques Bainville predicted most of the events which terminated with the catastrophe of 1939, without referring to the economic consequences of the war and the Treaty of Versailles. The rearming of Germany, the reoccupation of the Rhineland, the breakdown of alliances, of France with the successor-states of Austria-Hungary, the German-Russian alliance for the division of Poland, the German attack toward the west, the rupture of the German-Soviet pact, all these successive episodes of the drama evoke precedents and conform to the logic of power-politics. But, the Great Depression of 1929, the millions of unemployed, the complete disintegration of the political and economic unity of central Europe, was necessary in order for an emotional movement like National Socialism to succeed in mobilizing millions of Germans by giving them hope for the future. The diabolical genius of a Hitler was necessary in order for the desire for revenge to incarnate itself in a monstrous project and unheard-of crimes.

A battle for material was the form that a war between industrial societies inevitably must take. The Great Depression, however, was not the fatal consequence of the nature of these societies: we know that it would have been relatively easy to limit its ravages. But it was a dramatic accident, the possibility of which was created by the essence of our societies. Thirty years ago commentators would have denounced the misunderstanding of economic exigencies by the drafters of the Treaty of Versailles. Since 1945, a territorial status quo more irrational than that of 1918 does not exclude prosperity. Meanwhile, the Thirty Years' War has spawned consequences we have not finished meditating upon and about which we continue to ask: are they dramatic or necessary? dramatic and necessary? more necessary than dramatic?

These consequences (called by the Germans *weltgeschichtlich*) are well known: Europe has lost her preeminence. Yesterday the center of world politics, today she is divided into a zone where Soviet Russia reigns and a zone where the United States influence is dominant and which is defended by her strength. Colonial peoples have become independent. The industrialization which gave Europe its superiority has become or is becoming the common good of all mankind. With all the parts of the human race today (or tomorrow) disposing of the same instruments, is not the unremitting law of quantity going to apply to peace as well as war, reducing the old continent to the dimensions it occupies on the map?

"The withdrawal of Europe," "the decadence of Europe"—I have no doubt that the current configuration can be expressed in dramatic historical language. But, for us Europeans, who have suffered two great wars, known the worst outrages men have inflicted upon the honor of humanity, who acknowledge the end of empires, nothing is more tempting than morose meditation upon the fragility of historical works. But, must one give in to the temptation? The extension of industrial society, the unification of humanity, these two facts, provoked or accelerated by a "Thirty Years' War"—were they not inevitable, in keeping with the law of necessity? In the light of this, was not the entire drama, then, the means for the accomplishing of a destiny written in advance, the very one announced by August Comte: industrial society, exemplary for all human collectivities, creating, for the first time, the unity of all humanity?

Part III

Let us stop a moment and turn our attention to the other aspect of the century, towards the process of accumulation of knowledge and power. Economists and sociologists now are in the habit of studying the long-term movements of production and productivity. Following Colin Clark's *Conditions of Economic Progress*, the calculation of the growth rate (whether of the national product or per capita production of the population), the comparison of the *manpower* used in each of the sectors, has become a classic method for appreciating the development of different economies. But it is clear that national income statistics or those of employment reflect the results of dramatic events as much as a regular development. The diffusion of industry across the world has occurred by way of wars, revolutions and catastrophes.

This proposition is so little open to doubt that an illustration will suffice and a demonstration would be useless. Simply think about the completely different reactions China and Japan had to the influence and menace of the West. In Japan, it was a fraction of the ruling class which took the initiative for the historical mutation, without which the Empire of the Rising Sun was condemned to a sort of enslavement. In China, the great majority of the bureaucratic class was incapable either of understanding or realizing the necessary mutation, and a long period of civil wars and the Communist party's seizure of power were necessary for the Chinese state to have the strength and competence to execute an accelerated program of industrialization. Since 1890, the history of Asia has been a *décaloge* between the modernization of these two empires. It was the superiority acquired by borrowing means of power from the West that inspired Japan with the foolish ambition to conquer China. And it was the Sino-Japanese War which gave the best opportunity to the Communist party. In each case, at the beginning one will find a dramatic phase of conflict between the past and present, between tradition and the West.

The course of this dramatic phase determines not only the beginning and the pace of the process, it also contributes to the determination of the choice between possible methods: it decides which social group will take the initiative or the responsibility for it. In Japan, it was a class imbued with an aristocratic spirit which realized the mutation and attempted to preserve a synthesis of national values and Western techniques. In China, it was, finally, a class formed by Marxist-Leninist ideology and totalitarian practices which took charge of industrialization and the shaping and training of innumerable masses. Even in Russia, the *first steps* took place during the last quarter of the 19th century when absolutism continued to hold sway. The war and the revolution interrupted progress and caused a new elite to emerge which justified itself with a Western doctrine, but one which was opposed to the liberal West. Without the war of 1914, if customary history had not shook Czarism and given Lenin and his companions the occasion they had so long been looking for, one can conceive that the industrialization of Russia could have continued in another fashion, under the direction of another power, and at another pace. What seems to us inevitable, when we look at the past from our perspective in 1960, is that Russia, barring the destruction of her imperial unity from within or without, would have become the leading power of Europe. As soon as all peoples possess the same means of production and destruction, the law of numbers, within certain limits, comes into play. However, whatever answer we might give to these questions, it is legitimate to ask: what might have happened if Kerensky had eliminated the Bolshevik leaders during the aborted revolution of July 1917? What would have happened if Russia had benefited from two or three more decades of peace in order to overcome the crisis of the initial phase of industrialization?

If Russia did not receive the grace of this delay, if China was not spared from the ambitions of the more advanced countries of Asia, America, or Europe, it is not because the capitalist economies were inexorably devoted to imperialism, but rather because industrialization provided the means and excited the temptation of conquest and military glory. For statesmen and peoples who continued to think according to older categories, the main significance of industry was the growth of mobilizable resources. It did not open a new era, but instead gave supplementary cards in an ancient game.

It is here that, in a sense, history as usual and necessary history encounter each other: are knowledge and power, at the service of power-politics, or, as Auguste Comte prophesied, do they announce the end of power-politics, a unified humanity pursuing the only struggle worthwhile, that for the mastery of nature and the well-being of all men? The two great agitators of the 20th century, Japan and Germany, gave yesterday's response to today's question. Nothing has changed, the masters of these two empires thought, except for the number of soldiers and the effectiveness of weapons. Industry was a means of power and power's purpose was conquest. Is the same true today?

At the risk of being accused of making a naive claim, I will say that the current generation understands better than preceding ones the world in which we live, whose originality the thinkers of the last century had intuitively grasped. This optimism, it seems to me, is founded upon some facts.

The first, the best known, is the revolution in armaments. Between 1914 and 1945, the ability to destroy remained inferior to the capacity to produce and to construct. The armies of 1914 used weapons whose effectiveness was less than that which scientists and engineers would have been able to imagine and build if the best minds had devoted themselves to the task. The infantry of 1914, which moved by marching and horse-drawn cannon, belonged to tradition. Even armored divisions and air squadrons did not yet decisively overthrow cost-benefit analysis. The revolution dates from the nuclear explosion. A war conducted with thermonuclear bombs no longer would be rational for any of the belligerents. It is only since 1945 that industry has finally realized the first condition of peace by way of fear of war—an eventuality that so many writers had announced prematurely. It does not follow that peace is assured, but only that war no longer is the continuation of politics by other means. Thermonuclear war, except in circumstances of the near invulnerability of one of the belligerents, can only be the result of an accident or a misunderstanding.

In addition, world opinion more clearly than at any other time understands the nature of modern economic life and the pacific possibilities it contains. Between classes and peoples, the causes of conflict appear weaker than motives of solidarity. Certainly, there is nothing there that is fundamentally new. For centuries, liberal economists have affirmed that both parties gain in an exchange, that the essence of an economy is exchange, and that wars and conquests are always sterile and often ruinous for all.

But recent facts have contributed to the diffusion of these convictions once limited to narrow circles. West Germany, with a territory half the size of France, which had to absorb ten million refugees, experiences an unparalleled prosperity. The cost of defeat for it was not, as it would have been in the past, misery, but rather well-being. Western Europe as a whole, Great Britain included, has lost its colonies, its power, and its diplomatic prestige. However, it has never before reached a similar level of production and productivity. . . .

Does this mean that the industrial society, dreamed of by Auguste Comte and in the process of being actualized in various forms, truly is exemplary and that humanity is becoming socially uniform, as it is becoming diplomatically unified? Such a conclusion would be premature. The dawn of universal history, I believe, is about to begin. Universal history will exhibit certain original traits in contrast to the provincial histories of the nations or civilizations of the past six thousand years. Nothing, however, allows one to say that universal history will cease to be dramatic.

What do we want to suggest by the expression "universal history"? First of all, the unification of the diplomatic field. China and Japan, the Soviet Union and the United States, France and Great Britain, Germany and Italy, India and Ghana, all these states today belong to one and the same system. What happens on the coast of China is not without influence on relations between Europe and the United States or between the United States and the Soviet Union. Never have so many states recognized one another's right to exist; never have Europe, Asia, Africa, and America felt so close to each other. What the great states did once upon a time in Europe or Asia, today's great states—provisionally the United States and the Soviet Union—do across the five continents. It is trite to say that the means of communication and transportation have obliterated distance. The accumulation of means of knowledge and power in the continent-states is also one of the conditions of planetary diplomacy, of the changed scale of power.

The universal diffusion of certain forms of technical or economic organization accompanies diplomatic unification. No collectivity desiring to survive can refuse to develop productive forces—as the Marxists say, the rationalization of labor and the expansion of their technical apparatus. How can a collectivity refuse the means of power and well-being? Thus, the same airports, the same factories, the same machines strike the eyes of the visitor, from Tokyo to Paris, Beijing to Rio de Janeiro, and the same words—capitalism, communism, imperialism, dollar, ruble—sound in his ears as soon as he begins a conversation with an intellectual or politician. The traveler, if he remains on the level of these superficial impressions, can believe that humanity lives in a unitary world of machines and ideas.

Such impressions are largely illusory. Humanity, to the same extent as it is diplomatically unified, is as divided as all the diplomatic systems of the past. Two coalitions encounter and oppose one another in the center of Europe. Around them more and more states pride themselves on their non-alignment. Sino-Soviet relations are veiled in some mystery. The United Nations offers a symbolic tribunal for different nations' spokesmen, but most discourses express not the real weakness of states which condemns them to impotence, but an ideology employed to give themselves the feeling of participating in humanity's history. . . .

The reasons for the hostility between the factions of this unified humanity are not inhibited by any spiritual community. The unification has no other foundation than a material, technical, or economic one. The power of means of production, destruction, and communication has filled the oceans, leveled mountains, overcome distances. Vague ideologies, derived from European doctrines of the past century, furnish a few common words to men who do not adore the same gods, do not respect the same customs, do not think according to the same categories. Never have the states of a diplomatic system been so different, never the partners in the same project so devoid of profound solidarity.

For ten years or so we have been haunted by the great schism between the communist universe and the free world. How could it be otherwise, since Soviet armies are stationed two hundred kilometers from the Rhine and Soviet propaganda proclaims as inevitable the final, universal, triumph of communism—in other words, announces to the West that it has no other choice than that between being killed and dying naturally!

That is not all. The conflict between the two blocs has a dual character; it is a power-rivalry, but also an ideological competition—a foreign war—but it also exhibits certain traits of a civil war. Economic planning under proletarian guidance, for the purpose of abundance and equality: such a regime, whether realized or not in the Soviet Union, is a Western dream, a utopia, by way of negating the real, which, in the West, has dominated political (if not doctrinal) discussion for decades. Perhaps Orthodox Russia, heir of Byzantium and the monolithic traditions of oriental bureaucracy, belongs to another sphere of civilization. The Russia which claims Marxism and socialism belongs to the Western sphere of civilization, at least by the language it employs, and by the claim it makes to have accomplished what the best reformers of Europe themselves claimed to be humanity's goal.

Perhaps, too, the intensity of the conflict is waning. The irrationality of a war to the death carried on with thermonuclear weapons is obvious to the leaders of both blocs. The similarity of productive capacities and of the organization of labor, in industrial terms (whose juridical status differs), imposes itself, little by little, upon even minds the most captive to their preferred ideologies. Certainly, however, a place remains for genuine controversies. Differing in the status accorded to property, the mode of regulation applied to the entire economy, the style of authority, these societies are different in their ways of thinking and living. We ought not to repeat the error of certain Marxists by denying the repercussions of the economic regime on the ensemble of the societies, on the pretext of similarities, here and there, of productive forces and the organization of labor. This is no less an error than the one committed yesterday by the Bolsheviks of amplifying disproportionately the implications of the regimes: one, according to them, the guarantor of peace, equity, abundance; the other a fatal cause of imperialism, exploitation, and misery in the midst of an excessive accumulation of goods. We know how false these two mythical and contrasted views are. Let us not give in to the temptation of a new myth, which, though preferable to the older ones, would be no more true. The moral unity of mature industrial societies with different regimes is no more guaranteed than their conflict. Even if, as is probable, they resemble one another more and more, they would still not be essentially devoted to friendship. How many times in history have great wars seemed to be in retrospect wars of warring-brothers? . . .

To the extent that humanity henceforth lives a single history, it must acquire another rational mastery, not over its biological instincts but over social passions. The more that men of different races, religions, and customs live in the same world, the more they must show themselves capable of tolerance, of mutual respect. They mutually must recognize their humanity, without the ambition to reign or the will to conquer. No doubt these are banal formulae to which the reader will subscribe without effort. But let one reflect upon them: they require of man a virtue of a new kind. What most separates men from one another is what each one holds sacred. The pagan or the Jew who does not convert is an affront to a Christian. He who does not acknowledge the God of the religions of salvation, is he our kin or a stranger with whom we can have nothing in common? It is with him, too, that we will have to build a spiritual community, the superstructure or foundation of the material community which the unity of science, technology, and economy tends to create, a unity imposed by the historical destiny of a humanity more conscious of its quarrels than its solidarity.

The diplomatic field was unified through the drama of the two world wars. Industry expanded by the intermediary of the French, Russian, and Chinese revolutions. Violence blazed the way along which millions of innocent victims are strewn. The cunning of reason evoked by the disciples of Bossuet, Hegel, and Marx has not been economical with the sufferings and blood of men. Nothing proves that the times have evolved and that henceforth the rational process will continue without drama. It is possible that universal history could be different in this respect than the provincial histories of the past millennia. But that is only a hope, sustained by faith.

Conclusion

This sketch probably allows no other conclusion than the preceding formulation with its equivocation.

The philosophies of history accepted by our contemporaries place an emphasis on one or the other of the conjoined aspects of historical becoming. Optimistic philosophies, whether of liberal or Marxist inspiration, project indefinitely into the future the process of accumulation of knowledge and power. By the free market or by rational planning, all humanity will share equitably the benefits of a progress due to the genius of scientists or engineers. Pessimistic philosophies, such as Spengler's, note the similarities between the catastrophes which overcame past civilizations and those we have witnessed in the 20th century. Western civilization is dying, just as before it ancient civilization died, in wars and revolutions, sprawling cities and uprooted masses, in the sophistication of impotent elites and the triumph of money or technology. Is not a Europe which has lost its empires, already decadent? Does the transmission to other races of the instruments by which the white minority had assured its domination, mark the fatal degradation of Europe?

These philosophies, whether optimistic or pessimistic, misunderstand certain features of our time and the possibilities of the universal age. Interpreted in the light of the past, the old continent's present situation rightfully calls for morose meditation. What weight do yesterday's great powers, England, France, and Germany, with their fifty million men restless after well-being, have next to the continent-states whose standard measure is one hundred million? Have not the European nations, by losing their empires, lost, in a manner of speaking, their historical being, and must they not renounce grandeur? This traditional view is, perhaps, anachronistic. In our century, domination oftentimes costs more than it yields. Wealth has for its origin and measure rational, organized labor. Contemplating the world in the process of adopting the civilization to which it gave birth, Europe is not condemned to feel itself defeated by its victory. Grandeur is no longer necessarily linked with military power because the Great States are no longer able to use their weapons without provoking the reprisal of their own destruction, because no society any longer needs to rule over others in order to give its children honorable living conditions.

Europe has two reasons for refusing to indulge itself in a consciousness of decadence: it was Europe who, first of all by its works, then by its military follies, caused humanity to cross the threshold of the universal era. In this age when the exploitation of natural resources allows men no longer to tyrannize one another, Europe can be great by conforming itself to the spirit of the new times, by aiding other peoples to heal themselves of the infantile maladies of modernity. To realize its ideals within, to have a task to accomplish without: why should Europe continue to taste a bitterness the recent past explains but which is not justified by the prospects for the future?

Never have men had so many motives for not killing each other. Never have they had as many motives to feel themselves associated in one and the same project. I do not conclude from all this that the age of universal history will be peaceful. We know that man is a rational being, but what of men?

I conclude, at the end of a long excursus, with propositions the wisdom of nations would not deny. After having evoked Hegel and the cunning of reason, I find myself quite close to Candide and the language of Voltaire. But, after all, when philosophy (or sociology) rejoins common sense, is it homage to the latter or a guarantee of wisdom for the former?

Translated by Paul Seaton
with Daniel Mahoney

Notes

1. The First World War, 1914–1918, or as it was called before 1939, the "Great War." (Editor's note)

Part Five

Evaluating Modern Progress

Introduction

Faith without Illusions

Throughout this century, there has been much theoretical speculation about the "crisis" of liberal democracy. Aron was not closed to such speculation and he, as much as anyone, recognized that the twentieth century had witnessed grave theoretical and practical challenges to the survival and well-being of the liberal democratic regimes. An intellectually honest man, he did not deny *a priori* the view shared by penetrating thinkers of the left and the right, that a dialectic of modernity led inexorably to the weakening and even the self-destruction of liberal principles, that the political totalitarianisms and philosophical nihilisms of the twentieth century have a symbiotic relationship to the very liberalism that they reject.

But he saw no practical alternative to the liberal regime, no other regime which could find legitimacy with modern peoples. In his 1976 work, *In Defense of Decadent Europe*, he criticized the decline of civic spirit and martial virtue in liberal Europe and opposed a kind of libertarianism that attacked all institutions of authority, whether the army, university, or church. He had no respect for those who wanted to democratize every aspect of society by unionizing armies, politicizing universities and churches, and undermining deliberation in representative political institutions. However, he also refused to accept Alexander Solzhenitsyn's critique of the Enlightenment *in toto* or Oswald Spengler's gloom about the prospects for a free, mass, urban society. He defended, in an anxious but full-hearted and politic way, liberal and "decadent" Europe.

Aron's 1978 essay "For Progress" was originally published in one of the first issues of his quarterly review *Commentaire*. Beginning with a critique of the ex-Marxist, French "new philosophers" who had rather belatedly discovered the Gulag and proceeded to engage in haphazard and overdrawn political and philosophic speculations about its origins, Aron addresses the "crisis" of liberal democracy in light of the theo-

155

retical challenge to enlightenment principles from the left and right and the political challenge of communist totalitarianism. Despite genuine concern about the political vitality of the democracies, Aron ultimately reveals a democratic and "Kantian" faith in the vocation of mankind, a belief in the capacity of the human "conscience" to overcome the tyranny of the ideological lie and a totalitarian oligarchy. Aron's reasonable hopes that the experience of totalitarianism could restore substance and luster to the concept of the rights of man and reinvigorate the spirit of liberalism seems partially vindicated by the largely unforeseen but welcome collapse of communism. But the collapse of "hard" ideological despotism leaves what Alexis de Tocqueville called soft or "democratic despotism," nourished by political centralization, apathetic individualism, and the decline of civic spirit, as the most pressing danger to the integrity of our "pluralistic" societies. Aron both believed and hoped that Tocqueville had exaggerated fears of the likely or possible triumph of "democratic despotism." The strength of this essay lies precisely in Aron's ability to defend the dignity of liberal theory and practice while clearly recognizing the internally generated threats to its health, vigor, and well-being. For Aron, "progress" is not the result of an impersonal historical process but instead the hard-fought and never completely or eternally attained acquisition of moral agents "aspiring to (their) humanity." "For Progress" indicates that Aron remained in some limited but real sense a man of the (enlightenment) left. It remains for us, the citizens of the democracies today, to decide whether we can share Aron's qualified and sober faith in modern "progress." But Aron is undoubtedly correct: there is no viable or humane *political* alternative to constitutional democracy or modern technological progress available at the present time.

For Progress—After the Fall of the Idols

Raymond Aron

1978

Marx is not dead; in the secondary schools, in the *lycées*, even in the universities, he remains very much alive, an inexhaustible mine of quotations, concepts, and dogmas, an almost inevitable reference, if not an undisputed master. In England, sociologists have never read and discussed him so much. Althusser has disciples, almost a school there. He enjoys the same popularity in the United States. I open the June 29, 1978 issue of the *New York Review of Books*; I come across a remarkable article, "Inescapable Marx," by Robert L. Heilbroner, dedicated to an impressive list of books on Marx, his life, his theories of history and revolution, his heritage, and the meaning of his thought today—not to mention a magazine entitled, *Marxist Perspectives*, which reminds me of the collection of the 1930s, *In the Light of Marxism*.

Much of this work amounts to Marxology, rather than Marxism, although the majority of Marxists, even members of the Communist party, justify their position through an interpretation of the master. What distinguishes the "new philosophers" is the simultaneous condemnation of Marx, Gulag, and the Soviet Union (even if they also have to condemn capitalism and socialism at the same time). A fraction of the high—or presumably high—level Parisian *intelligentsia*, today as yesterday, does not distinguish between Marx and the Soviet Union with an inverted accent of value. The approach of hell is replacing the hope of paradise.

Alexis de Tocqueville had foreseen that the superficial agitation of democratic society would not spare intellectual life. Paris is the capital of fashionable ideas, no less than fashion. *Gurus* are revered for a few years or months, make their rounds and then move on. The new gurus who kill the gods of yesterday are not fundamentally different from the *gurus* of the 1950s or 1960s. Whether one discovers a structuralist Marx or excommunicates the philosophers of German idealism by dint of collages of quotations amounts to the same thing in practice. The style changes, the talent varies; sometimes the good news—the 1977 vintage guaranteed—reaches the general public and the international weeklies; later the sect returns to the obscurity from which the press had snatched it.

Does the present moment—the death of Marx by and for "the princes of intelligence"—have a different historical significance from the preceding ones, the quarrelsome association between the existentialists and the communists, the Camus–Sartre–Merleau-Ponty debates, the rise of Louis Althusser and his decline, the Maoists in Paris? I hesitate to answer. The books that reveal the truth of the day do not seem to me, as works of thought, superior to those of the recent past. Quite the opposite. But I do not trust my judgment, because of my probable bias in favor of the men of my generation.

Moreover, it matters little. What interests me is that a prolonged phase of economic crisis coincides, not with a revival of Marxism, but, at least in appearance, with a completely opposite reaction. The delayed recognition, under the influence of Solzhenitsyn, of Soviet reality has provoked a sort of total rejection in some people, not only of Marx, Marxism, and the Soviet Union, but of the master thinkers of modern civilization. The ambition of philosophers to change the world by interpreting it is becoming the primal sin, and, since its source was historical materialism, we find these young people ready to charge intellectuals and their optimism with all the crimes of the century, from the slaughters at Verdun to Gulag—a word emptied of meaning by misuse. Even the Bastille of Louis XIV is baptized "Gulag."

Radiant socialism in opposition to sordid capitalism? There is no longer any question of it: both of them, avatars of the same capital, would show two barely different faces of the same barbarism. Let us read a few lines from the book that enjoyed remarkable success.

> It is therefore meaningless to "criticize" the idea of progress. It is also meaningless to attack its "illusions." And it is meaningless again to set up other mechanisms and other real processes in opposition to it. We must believe in progress, believe in its infinite power, and grant it all the credit it asks for. But we must simply denounce it as a reactionary mechanism which is leading the world to catastrophe. We have to say what it says, see the world as it does, record the signs of its devastation wherever it rules. And it is precisely for that reason that we must discredit it, and only in that sense that it must be analyzed, as a uniform and linear progression toward evil. No, the world is not wandering nor lost in meanders of possibility. It is heading straight for uniformity, the shallows, the mean. And in order to protest against that, now, for the first time, we must proclaim ourselves *antiprogressive*.[1]

This sort of prophecy defies the old practice, dear to French education, of the *explication de texte*. Progress, I suppose, designates economic development, more or less identified with science, technology, and industrialization. Has this progress become reactionary? How? Why? Is it a one-way road to Evil? What Evil? Is it leading the world to catastrophe? What catastrophe? The catastrophe foreseen by the Club of Rome? Is it producing uniformity, leveling, and mediocrity? Leveling or mediocrity? There is no longer any choice or hope. Progress, like Marxism, leads inexorably to catastrophe, but, in distinction to Marxism, it promises no after-catastrophe.

To this abdication before a mysterious and pitiless destiny, I still prefer the optimism of the rationalists of the recent past. The eloquent and naive voices that irritated me so much a half century ago are recovering some freshness for me.

> The history of human industry is rightly the history of civilization and vice versa. The propagation and discovery of the industrial arts both was and still is fundamental progress. It permitted a happier and happier life for ever greater masses over ever vaster territories. It was the industrial arts, through the development of ideas and societies, that made possible the development of reason, sensibility, and will. It was the industrial arts that made modern man the most perfect of animals. The industrial arts are the Prometheus of ancient drama. Keeping them in mind, let us read the magnificent verses of Aeschylus and let us say that it was the industrial arts that made men out of those weak ants that haunted dark caves, out of those children who did not see what they saw, did not understand what they heard, and who, throughout their lives, blurred their images with the phantoms of their dreams. . . . Beyond any doubt, it will be the industrial arts that will save humanity from the moral and material crisis in which it is struggling. Science and industry are superior to fate rather than subject to it. They are the third God that is putting an end to the gods, to the tyrants of heaven and earth. . . . [2]

As soon as I left the sheltered little world of the university, I collided with the calamity of the Germans, their nationalistic delirium. I revolted against the faith of these men of good will; I no longer shared their confidence in the capacity of science to save humanity from its moral and material crisis. To reflect on the course of human history is to become conscious of the human condition, of an incoherent world, torn by conflicts among classes, nations, and ideologies. A dramatic condition that forbids immoderate hopes but does not justify resignation.

Forty years ago, I meditated on history in the shadow of the Great

Depression, my glance turned toward World War II, whose warning symptoms only the blind did not perceive. Today I am writing in the shadow of an economic crisis, completely different from that of the 1930s. The "undiscoverable" war, the war of Superpowers, remains improbable. Ever since the cultural revolt of the 1930s, however, modern civilization in its entirety has been on trial. If socialism is no better than capitalism, where does the blame fall if not on science, progress, technology, and, indeed, economic development? An accusation as old as the accused: Rousseau against the Encyclopedists; the counterrevolutionaries against the Enlightenment and the Revolution; Nietzsche against the petty bourgeoisie or socialism. Was it with the Renaissance, the Age of Enlightenment, or in 1789, at the time of the French Revolution, that the West took the fatal turn? I leave to others this historical trial and its verdict.

Today there is no longer any point in unmasking Marxist mystifications. It is nihilism, the opposite of the Marxism of yesterday, one has to denounce today. The death of Marxism or the defeat of the left threatens to carry off hope as well. As early as twenty years ago, Maurice Merleau-Ponty wrote that Marxism was not one philosophy of history among others, but historical Reason itself—which he condemned along with Marxism. A generation later, the same line of argument goes even further. The failure of Marxism would reveal modern civilization in its entirety as irresistible progress toward Evil. We who remain faithful to democracy, science, and liberalism, let us accept the challenge. Let us have no polemics, but begin to examine our consciences.

Let us think back to the years immediately following the war. No one raised his voice against growth or industrialization, either on the left or the right. The left blamed the Malthusianism of French bosses. Statisticians compared the number of persons nourished by the French peasant and by the American farmer. For years, the Soviet growth rate challenged West Europeans. Ordinarily more clairvoyant, many economists foresaw the imminent lowering of the Iron Curtain by Westerners themselves, incapable of bearing the comparison between the lot of the workers in France and that of the liberated proletarians to the East.

If the French economy had not kept pace in the race, or if it had progressed in the manner of Great Britain—that is, half as fast as the German Federal Republic—the French, in their humiliation, would again, as they did in 1938, denounce the inefficiency of capitalism and capitalists. After the war, we had no other choice than to give up forever or to renew our old structures through science, technology, or industry.

A nation that was one of the greatest in Europe, and which still desires to maintain its rank in the world, had to submit to the imperatives of work and productivity. (Let us say progress if others prefer the word.) Are we to call this kind of progress "reaction"? Quite evidently, it does not lead us backwards, it leads us toward a society without precedent—a society that no one is forced to prefer to those of the past. But toward which societies of the past are we to turn our glances and regrets?

Those who knew the France of 1938 do not miss it: the condition of the worker was incomparably harsher, and peasant life was narrower and more painful; only the children of the bourgeoisie and a few hundred or thousand scholarship-holders had access to secondary and higher education; the establishment jealously guarded its powers and privileges; more closed in on itself than ever, France was unaware of the universe and feared the future, Germany and war.

Do we wish to go back further, to the France of the peasants who elected Napoleon III by plebiscite? Or had those Frenchmen, 80 percent of whom lived still in the countryside or little towns, already been wounded by "progress," because the intellectuals believed in the Enlightenment, and because individuals no longer accepted, as a decree of God or nature, their place in society or the established order? I do not believe that those who call progress "reaction" go so far as to eliminate, in their nostalgia, the equality of individuals before the law, the citizenship of all, as formal as it may be, and, with them, the liberties that were baptized the rights of man.

Promethean ambition and the rights of man (or universal citizenship) have nothing in common, one will probably object. Logically, the objection is valid. The will to become master and possessor of nature in no way explains the participation of all in the government of the city and the respect for individuals. But, historically, these two movements of ideas and events are interrelated. Learned men are eroding the prestige of men of quality or birth. Certainly, Jean-Jacques Rousseau observed or foresaw the corruption of morals by the arts and sciences; citizens as he conceived them, poor and virtuous, do not resemble those of today—producers, consumers, taxpayers, and television viewers. The Encyclopedists and Saint-Simonians both applauded the future, our present, of which they had a presentiment. Rousseau detested it in advance; he liked the *Ancien Régime* no better. Civil liberties, in an austere city—a dream on the edge of the historically possible.

I would not, however, say that progress, as it is unfolding, leaves no way out. If we suppose that progress embraces "science, technology, and economic development," it is absurd to decree it "a one-way road to Evil." If, in their recovery from ideology, these philosophers will no longer permit the sacrifice of the humble to the constructions of the master thinkers, why do they forget that the science that produced the bombs and nuclear centers also eliminated epidemics and, for the majority of mankind, famine?

Goats have devastated the terrain of civilizations more often than pollution. And knowledge has a greater chance of arresting the spread of the desert in the Sahel than prayers to the gods and invectives against science. I am ashamed of these remarks, worthy of Mr. Homais, but those who beat their *mea culpa* on the chests of others and replace their delirium of yesterday with another, opposite in kind, arouse my bile from time to time. There is no good, in history, that does not include a share of evil. The least costly and most effective investments are perhaps those of hygiene. They save millions of lives; they do not assure the means of living decently. Teaching every child to read and write does not suffice to elevate him to culture. Are we to prefer the illiterate to the semi-cultivated? Are we to prefer the peasant who, a century ago, hardly left his village, to the agricultural producer of today who drives a tractor, knows the world through television, and whose daughters desire an urban style of living?

Understand me well: I take the quarrel with industrial society seriously, whether it comes from the Club of Rome (shortage of energy, nonrenewable resources, and pollution) or from thinkers who fear the deterioration of man or of the quality of life. Serious questions call for inquiries and answers. What I am attacking is cheap pessimism, historical fatalism, and "irresistible progress toward Evil."

Toward what "evil" is "progress" leading us? War, totalitarianism, concentration camps, mediocrity, or egalitarianism? The wars of the nineteenth century were bloodier than most wars of the past, but, at the same time, they have left fewer traces from a material standpoint. In 1920, Spanish influenza wiped out the lives of about ten million people, as many as the war. The voids were rapidly filled and no population was bled as that of Germany during the Thirty Years' War (reduced by half). Perhaps, in terms of percentage of population, losses in combat have risen in the twentieth century. Some estimate at a million the number of Algerian victims between 1955 and 1962. The Algerian people today exceed fifteen million. At the time of the conquest, Algeria numbered two or three million souls. Must we weep for the dead of the conquest and the liberation? Yes. Must we imagine what Algeria would be today if the French had not conquered it in the preceding century? That would be an exercise in *counterfactu-*

al history, devoid of meaning. No one can answer. How can we compare the evils inflicted to the benefits disseminated, even involuntarily?

Wars always assume the form of the societies from which they emanate. Weapons depend on industry; military organization depends both on social organization and on weapons. In 1914, universal suffrage was in accord with conscription; weapons, still relatively simple, permitted the mobilization of millions of combatants. The growing cost of arms now tends to reduce the number of combatants. Some of them, the pilots, need gunner-mates. We are free to prefer other military institutions, for example, those of the *Ancien Régime*, with the recruitment of officers from the nobility, and of simple soldiers from the lowest classes of society. If we condemn war on moral grounds, we must condemn it also when politico-technological circumstances limit its ravages.

War, the settling of conflicts among political entities by force, is not an invention of modern civilization. Democracy, nationalism, technology, and science make possible the mobilization of millions of men, the manufacture of tens of thousands of cannons, and wars of peoples and of propaganda. But the same capacity to produce and act in common permits the reconstruction of material ruins in a few years. Let us compare the Western Europe of 1955—ten years after the end of the Third Reich—with that of 1935; aside from the concentration camps, tombs, and the massacre of the innocents, the Europeans of the West found themselves freer, less divided, and more prosperous than twenty years earlier.

A materialistic and cynical reckoning? I agree. Each person is "unique and irreplaceable." How many Menuhins perished at Auschwitz before revealing their genius? How many Cavailles or Lautmans whose deaths deprived humanity of the works they bore within them? Who can forget? Who can forgive? But neither history nor the species, judging from the experience of centuries, cares about individuals. As for peoples, the decline in the birth rate threatens them with extinction more than war—with the exception of the Holocaust, which is without parallel. Conquerors have more than once run their swords through hundreds of thousands of men, women, and children, but never was the extermination of a human group conceived cold-bloodedly, never organized and executed so methodically, and, I dare say, so rationally.

Are we to incriminate rationality, because it can be made to serve life and death indiscriminately? Similar methods of organization apply to the movement of armored divisions and of drivers on vacation, to concentration camps and to the camps of the Club Méditerranée.

No, rational organization does not bear its soul within itself. In a famous lecture, at the 1965 Congress in Heidelberg, to commemorate the hundredth anniversary of the birth of Max Weber, Herbert Marcuse denounced the distinction between formal and substantial rationality, or more precisely, the incompatibility between the two. He denounced "the neutrality of technical reason with regard to all external affirmations of substantial values."

Marcuse imagines the reconciliation of formal and substantial rationality in automated production, which would liberate man from socially necessary but dehumanizing work. Until today, he admits, Max Weber has had the last word. The rational organization of production does not, as such, determine its goals: private or public, production serves ends imposed upon it from without. And rational bureaucracy risks being subjected to the irrationality of a charismatic leader.

According to Marcuse's criticism, Max Weber had at the outset assumed private enterprise and the market, along with *das Gehäuse der Gehörigkeit*, that is, the edifice of powers or the servitude of the majority. The experiments with public enterprises and planning have all crystallized *das Gehäuse der Gehörigkeit*. It is therefore, Marcuse, argues, necessary to imagine enterprises that would remain efficient without the separation of labor and management, or even to imagine automation that would combine formal and substantial rationality without submitting it to political, and therefore, often irrational, will.

Herbert Marcuse's polemic against Weberian rationality, which was acclaimed in 1965, reminds us of the debates of the Weimar Republic. Capitalism or socialism, privately or publicly owned property, the market or planning: these antitheses set the terms of debate and discussion at that time. But now the demystification of Soviet reality strips the old notion of the nationalization of the means of production of its charms. Utopia has to be sought at the farthest reaches of progress in a technology that is liberating in its own right—and even then data processing occasions nightmares as well as rosy dreams.

The case *against* rationalism turns easily into the case against totalitarianism. Do not the means of communication figure among the conditions indispensable to totalitarianism? Only those regimes deserve to be called totalitarian in which a single party holds a monopoly of activity or political legitimacy—a party that professes an ideology: that the State decrees a political, indeed a human, truth. The Soviet regime comes closest to the perfect example, because, in the name of atheism and materialism, it combats the faith of the Church, the Christian religion. The claim of the State-party to possess the supreme truth explains the monopolization of the means of communication. The State ideology must not, in the main, be called into question.

Does such a regime require radio and television? The founders of the Soviet State, Lenin and his companions, had neither at their disposal. Marxist-Leninist fanaticism, the kind that animated Lenin and his companions, characterizes certain features of our civilization; it presupposes the weakening of transcendent faith, the de-Christianization of the masses; perhaps the pseudo-science of Marxism borrows its authority from the cult of true science. Even Hitler's racism covered itself in scientific ragged finery. In this sense, these totalitarian ideologies have some affinity with modern civilization. They caricature science at the same time that they mimic religion or the Church. Toynbee defined Marxism more than once as a Christian heresy: the proletariat will save humanity; the most disinherited will rise to the top for the good of all; the way of the cross—"the class struggle"—will end with the reconciliation of men with one another and with nature. Alain Besançon interprets Leninism as a gnosis, with the perfect ones (the party) confident in their election and in the abyss between them and the others, between the corrupt world and the world that will emerge from the revolution.

I doubt that any century has been spared the superstitions and sects that swarm around Churches. The media did perhaps facilitate Hitler's rise to power; Lenin owes his victory above all to the war. Totalitarian ideologies (I am thinking of Marxism and its derivatives) mingle half-truths, vestiges of Christianity, ancestral dreams, and scraps of science and science-fiction. As for the techniques of communication, they do not seem to me to be either the origin or the supporting pillar of totalitarian regimes (as is often said). Of course, they provide power with additional instruments; they make it possible to mislead crowds, to broadcast the litanies of the State's truth or philippics against the eternal, forever elusive enemy, capitalism or imperialism, to the last village and into the brush. But before television or the computer, the police, denunciations, and bureaucracies functioned with pen and paper.

I even wonder, at the risk of paradox, whether State propaganda does not bring saturation and, indeed, provoke rejection. Hitler did succeed in casting a spell over crowds with his voice—but not Stalin, hidden in the Kremlin and in his cunning. After the attack of the Nazi armies, when he finally brought himself to address the country, he appealed to perennial sentiments, to patriotism, to the defense of Holy Russia. In the countries of Eastern Europe, not even governments dare to use stiff, emotionless language any longer. In Hungary, the scaffolding, mounted in ten years by the conquerors and their servants, collapsed in a few days in the year 1956, and free of a carapace of lies the Hungarians came to themselves. In an even more spectacular, non-violent manner, in Czechoslovakia twelve years later, the truth broke out in a storm. In spite of all technical means, the State had not convinced its subjects. Perhaps millions of men had lived in two universes at the same time: the universe of the official truth that they heard, and the universe of the other truth that they harbored deep inside themselves without even knowing it.

Was the totalitarian outcome in some way predetermined by the intellectual origins of modernity? If the answer is "yes," the Enlightenment, liberalism, capitalism, socialism—those moments of thought and of Western history—would form a necessary sequence and the verdict is final. I myself wrote the following words that I have not yet retracted:

> The philosophy of the Enlightenment, liberalism, naturally, if not necessarily, ends in socialism, indeed, in Marxism, just as rivers end in the sea.

Words probably dictated to me by Montesquieu's formula: monarchies tend toward despotism. In appearance, nothing is more contrary than the thought of the Enlightenment, of Montesquieu or of Voltaire, to socialism or Marxism. By what route did Spengler, and many others with him, embrace, in a single historical movement, the Enlightenment, liberalism, and socialism? Simplified to the point of risking caricature, the path is traced as follows.

The philosophy of the Enlightenment exalts reason and even individual reason; it destroys the authority of the Church and, at the same time, the authority of religion, although belief in a clock-god or a vague theism survives. It is an optimistic philosophy, which preaches the education of the human race, roots out superstitions, and places trust in science. The liberalism of the economist accords with the inspiration of the Enlightenment; the image of an organic society—each of the *states* or persons occupying an appropriate position, and together forming a coherent and hierarchical whole—gives way to a completely different image: a society constantly agitated by thousands and thousands of individuals in pursuit of their interests, wealth, and advancement. These individuals no longer obey higher authority, whether God or legitimate or semi-sacralized powers.

Once man has rejected masters and gods, once all possess the same right to happiness, socialism dogs liberalism. For a long time biological analogies (the survival of the fittest) or the invisible hand (from the clash of egoisms emerges what is best for all) justified economic liberalism. For a long time political liberalism sought justification in the efficacy of dialogue: by exchanging opinions, by bringing together their knowledge, citizens would arrive at the truth or right decision. But the argument continues: what remains of the utilitarian or rationalist foundation of liberalism? Free competition among individuals does not assure the rise of the fittest: the starting points are too unequal. Qualities that favor success are not those that inspire respect and obedience. In commercial or electoral competition, victory does not of itself turn the victor to *un homme de qualité*—unless public opinion considers success a criterion of worth. Once success is taken to be arbitrary or unfair, the less favored will demand not so much the right to the pursuit of happiness as the guarantee of a piece of it.

Political debates focus more and more on the national product and its distribution. The richer the societies, the more bitter the struggle for the standard of living. Can our civilization rise above the alternative of commerce or tyranny? Or is it actually in the throes of both extremes which it falsely sets in opposition? The commercial and monetary order of the West means also multi-national corporations, tentacular bureaucracies. "Prometheus putting an end to the tyrants of heaven and earth?" Yes, perhaps, but perhaps also:

> No one knows who will live in this edifice; whether at the end of this transformation entirely new prophets will emerge; whether the old ideas and ideals of yesterday will regain new vigor, or whether, on the contrary, a mechanical petrification, adorned in its shrivelled importance, will prevail. In that case, for the "last men" in this evolution of culture, the following words would become true: soulless specialists, heartless men of pleasure; this nothingness boasts of reaching a summit of humanity never yet attained. (Max Weber)

Let us abandon these distant perspectives. Promethean and organized, our societies continue to contain *das Gehäuse der Gehörigkeit*, the structure of material production and bureaucracy in which more than 80 percent of the population—the wage-earners—spend their working hours. Outside of this edifice, do not our societies resemble Tocqueville's vision: family cells, exclusively concerned with their little affairs, reading the same books, watching the same programs on television, unaware of, and yet imitating, each other.

> I see a countless crowd of similar and equal men on treadmills, in pursuit of vulgar little pleasures with which they fill their souls. Each man, aloof, is like a stranger to the destinies of all the others: his own children and personal friends constitute the whole human race for him; as for the rest of his fellow-citizens, he is next to them but does not see them;

he touches them but does not feel them; he exists only in himself and
for himself alone, and, if he still has a family, we can at least say that
he no longer has a country.

How many times this text has been cited as proof of the prescience
of Tocqueville! Let us translate into sociological jargon: the nuclear
family, the narrow horizon of the petty bourgeois, egoism set up as
the norm of life—in short, a hardened humanity, a swarm of mediocre men, each concerned with himself and unaware of his nothingness. What does their number matter, since all are cut on the same
model? How much they resemble one another without knowing it! The
same scorn came of Nietzsche's pen a few decades later. Less blinded
by hatred of capitalism than Marx, too aristocratic to love the democracy of the *common man*, both Tocqueville and Nietzsche saw the rise
of the class whose numbers economic progress was to inflate. Let us
call this class the petty bourgeoisie, which ranges from the most skilled
workers to average white-collar employees. The peasantry is disap-
pearing; what remains of it is being transformed into wheat and meat
producers—into machine operators. Are we to condemn this society
without precedent, whose urban style reaches into what used to be
called the country, this society that is striving to teach all its children
to read and write? In the name of what are we to condemn it?

Did the peasants that Balzac described represent a human type
superior to our farmers who know how to draw up the budget of their
enterprises and how to respond to the market? Are white-collar workers victims of progress? Can we call progress "reaction" when this
progress reduces the number of blue-collar employees; when it multiplies middle-class wage-earners, those who deal with figures and sym-
bols, and reduces the number of paid laborers, those who grapple with
matter? What right do we have to scorn these ordinary men? Who has
the right to scorn them? Faced with these kinds of questions, I feel
paralyzed. One man says the great majority will, of course, be mediocre. Another says the few will save humanity. He goes on to say, I
prefer the wisdom of the illiterate peasant to the semi-cultivated, who
catch, in passing, at bits of ideas, at the favorite phrases of journalists, and discuss the world's future.

Civilizations have always had an aristocracy of thought, if not of
position. Today, it is the scholars, the authentic scholars, who constitute, along with the great artists, the aristocracy of the aristocracy.
But these aristocrats do not offer a model of how to be a man that
other men would try to imitate. As for those surrounded by the clam-
our of popularity and considered the privileged *par excellence* (from

singers, movie actors, or writers, to corporation executives or government ministers), they permit millions of fans vicariously to live prestigious lives, but they themselves have almost nothing in common, and do not teach the same lesson.

I wonder whether Tocqueville's two affirmations are self-evident. In what way do men of our societies resemble one another more today than yesterday? Do they know less about their fellow men, their neighbors, and their country than our ancestors? Universal education has suppressed dialects. The customs of cities are spreading to the countryside, and city-dwellers are buying the old furniture that villagers replace with Grand Rapids. This sort of homogeneity of language maintained by the diffusion of the same words, of a few fashionable ideas, hides entirely different existences. Did villagers once differ from one another more than office workers do today? Were the habitués of the court of Louis XIV, as we know them from Saint-Simon, better than the courtiers of the President of the Republic or the president of a corporation?

Close-knit families, near their peasant origins and still far from the fashionable neighborhoods, differ from their parents or grandparents less in the narrowness of their life styles than in their ambition. The curse (or merit) of modern civilization is to shake the rules of tradition and the inheritance of trade and status, to make parents aware of social competition, of the opportunity for some to rise and of the risk that others will fall. Even if social mobility is less than our ideals suggest, it dominates the thought and conduct of families. It creates the obsession for education and, at the same time, it makes disappointments inevitable. Not all the young can win in either the genetic or the social lottery.

Endowed with consciousness, and therefore aware of their interests, have these atoms lost their country, and are they, as Tocqueville foresaw, concerned exclusively with their well-being? Certainly, our civilization tends toward a utilitarian or hedonistic morality. Who still evokes the categorical imperative? To the superficial observer, everything in our Western societies happens as if the distribution of the national income constituted the only stake in political quarrels, as if citizens no longer conceived any goal other than the improvement of their standard of living.

This impression rests on well-founded illusion and, to some extent, on reality. But the "materialism" of democratic politics is the result of the separation of religion from the State, and of ideology from the State. Lay or neutral, the State does not give citizens reasons for living. It leaves to individuals the freedom or the burden of finding them of themselves. The partisan State, whether Soviet or Nazi, broadcasts a message, sometimes arouses enthusiasm and devotion, presents itself as "idealistic," and indulges in murder. Is there less authentic "idealism" in the commercial societies of the West than in the tyrannical societies of the East? Solzhenitsyn detests slovenliness, sexual license, the noise and vulgarity of public life or of the press in the West. But he does not confuse these evils with Evil *par excellence*, namely, the absence of law and the institutional lie of totalitarianism. He does not announce, as predestined, the triumph of Evil, and the fall of the West.

I belong to the school of thought that Solzhenitsyn calls rational humanism, and says has failed. This rationalism does not imply certain of the intellectual or moral errors that Solzhenitsyn attributes to it. Montesquieu maintains a balance between the Eurocentrism of the Enlightenment and historicism. Science's universal vocation is not incompatible with a diversity of cultures. It is the leaders of the Third World who desire the spread of Western technology throughout the entire planet. Who refuses the instruments of power and wealth? Now become the Far West, Japan will perhaps better safeguard her identity than other countries whose masters would like to separate machines from the thought which makes them possible.

In what sense can we decree the failure of rational humanism? The rationalist is not unaware of the animal impulses in man, and of the passions of man in society. The rationalist has long since abandoned the illusion that men, alone or in groups, are reasonable. He bets on the education of humanity, even if he is not sure he will win his wager.

The West has ventured further than any other civilization in pursuit of the moral and intellectual freedom of the individual—a freedom in apparent contradiction with the structure of organizations, *das Gehäuse der Gehörigkeit*. There is a growing discordance between the culture of the West and its economic institutions.

Pitilessly, Solzhenitsyn notes the symptoms of weakness of the West, and finds their profound cause to be the eradication of faith. "In itself, the turning point of the Renaissance was ineluctable, the Middle Ages had exhausted its possibilities, the despotic crushing of the physical nature of man to the benefit of his spiritual nature had become unbearable. But, this time, we leapt from the *Spirit* to matter, in a disproportionate and exaggerated manner."

The history of Europe, since the Renaissance, is full of adventures and battles that only a simplistic Marxist would reduce to the passion for profit or the love of gold. Religious wars and wars of the French Revolution witness more to men's attachment to truth as they see it than to an exclusive concern for money and comfort. In the final analysis, Solzhenitsyn reproaches the West for its loss of Christian faith, where Tocqueville, after the fall of the *Ancien Régime* saw and foresaw societies stirred more and more by the envious and universal pursuit of well-being.

To reproach a person or a society for having lost faith seems as ridiculous to me as calling a believer "still a prisoner of superstitions." The rationalist of today is not unaware of the limits of scientific knowledge. He neither scorns nor condemns those who populate the world beyond knowledge with the images of their faith or the ideas of their intelligence. He does, however, condemn ideologies with totalistic pretensions, ideologies which are but poor replicas of religions that once gave a civilization a deep unity. The clericalism that had to be fought yesterday now assumes the form of the partisan State or of State ideology. At least initially, the totalizing ideology calls for devotion, sacrifices, and self-abnegation on the part of the faithful or militants. Are the young people who followed Hitler—young people whom I knew in 1931—and even a number of today's communists to be called idealists?

Neither the historian nor the philosopher, and even less the futurologist, possesses the answer to the questions that the West—and, in particular, Western Europe—is asking itself. Can a civilization prosper without a faith shared by the great majority? Will individuals tolerate the moral desert from which they are suffering and for which they reproach "society," that elusive entity that is blamed for everything including the crimes individuals commit? Many intellectuals are enraged by capital punishment, though murderers, thugs or political commissars once did, and sometimes still do, leave them indifferent or indulgent. In the name of ideas, terrorists usurp the right to execute—a right the state is no longer supposed to exercise. The liberal applauds the desacralization of the State; he is uneasy at the contempt displayed for laws, for he knows that without laws men cannot live together peaceably. He is disturbed too at the contradictions of the loudest, roughest and most widely-listened-to speakers of the market place—speakers who expose power and attack it wherever it still exists and who, at the same time, advocate the immunity of the individual who is to be sole master of himself. At what point of the disintegration of the State will men be held accountable for their acts?

Certainly, individuals are molded by their families, their social milieu, by chance encounters, and by the schools they happen to attend. Regardless of the strength or weakness of the State, individuals interiorize the norms of the city and draw a winning or losing number at the social lottery. In Western societies, they still, nevertheless, have the opportunity to fashion their characters in the benignity of liberty, and not at the risk of liberty or life in defiance of official truth.

The European nations have populated the New World; they have spread their science and their weapons of production and destruction across five continents, but have not, for all that, converted the other civilizations to their true gods. (Europe has had greater success with its idols.) In one sense, Europeans have exhausted the historical mission which Auguste Comte or Karl Marx, in a different sense, entrusted to them at the beginning of the last century. Because the passions that set them against one another almost destroyed them, they even doubt the words for which their grandfathers endured four years of martyrdom in 1914–18. Today, Gulag, the emblem of total tyranny in the name of total liberation, weighs, a remorse and a threat, on Communist parties (at least in Western Europe) and paralyzes mass ideological movements of the left or the right. The memory of Hitler and the persistence of Soviet totalitarianism do not protect the European West from its own demons: workers revolt against the rationalization of production, against the uprooting of communities that are the victims of economic growth, and against the disintegration of society under an invading State. Better than any other, the Italian people can survive without a State and in a kind of anarchy. But for the Italian people also, there are limits to patience—limits that France or Germany would rapidly reach.

With their mission accomplished (on the assumption that this teleological or quasi-theological language is acceptable), have the European nations no longer anything to say or do? Are they condemned to vegetate in the mediocrity of comfort and of the middle class, slaves of progress-reaction? Drawn into themselves, half-united for the purpose of prosperity but incapable of acting together on the world-stage, will they submit willingly or be forced to submit to an Empire which utilizes science but disowns its inspiration? An Empire at once despotic and ideocratic that will at all costs combine scientific method in arms production with a pseudo-scientific superstition in order to perpetuate an omnipotent oligarchy?

In spite of everything, "progress" leaves us with one hope. Despotism requires an educated work force: scientists, engineers. It cannot close its borders to radio and television, to the images coming from the world outside. To be sure, data processing will permit control of the entire population, individual by individual—it makes possible the nightmare of *1984*. But Europe's progress has not been solely or essentially that of machines; it has also been the progress of science and individuals. Thanks to Prometheanism, a growing portion of the population is gaining access to the opportunities of liberty.

The pressure of technical rationalization and the religious desert incite and renew revolts. Are Europeans perhaps better immunized against the totalitarian temptation than others? More and more isolated within a league of States that scorn the rights of man as we conceive them, in action and often in thought, Europeans appear weak in the face of the totalitarian empire. But they retain a strength that Solzhenitsyn underestimates, the strength of liberalism, tried and vigorous, which rests on no foundation other than the conscience of the individual.

Perhaps Spengler is right, and pitiless decadence is striking at formless and godless urban and commercial civilizations. Perhaps Toynbee is right to hope for a Christian and even a Catholic revival to rescue the West from the final fall toward which it is moving. The forecasts of historians are no more certain than the prophecies of sooth-sayers. Science and economic prosperity have given societies the means to enlarge their circle of citizens. The ideas of the Enlightenment that stem from the Greco-Christian tradition are still alive in the theory of the rights of man. They recover their lustre and youth in the experience of revolutions.

Reason "will not put an end to the tyrants of heaven and earth," but her struggle with them will endure as long as a strange animal species keeps aspiring to humanity.

Translated by Violet M. Horvath

Notes

1. B. H. Lévy, *Barbarism with a Human Face* (New York: 1979), p. 130.
2. These are the words of Marcel Mauss.

Appendix

On Tocqueville

Raymond Aron

1980

As an observer of his own country, Tocqueville formulated one of the great problems of our history, a problem that has been with us now for two centuries.[1] What do administrative centralism and the procedures of a representative regime consist of in a country of ancient monarchy? Can the French people arrive at a fully legitimate regime to which the citizens will adhere unanimously? Or is France, lacking a local democracy at the root of public life and torn by so many tragic memories and incompatible loyalties, still subject to sudden crises which are more spectacular than they are profound since the power elites come and go while the bureaucratic structure remains in place?

Perhaps a change has taken place with the establishment of the Fifth Republic. The Constitution draws its inspiration from both the monarchical and the republican traditions. In 1968 the French may well have proven that democracy had vindicated its claim to legitimacy. The response to upheaval this time was not revolution, but rather elections.

Much more than that, for the first time the President of the Republic and the Minister of Justice willingly appealed to Alexis de Tocqueville.[2] Is the new political science which he sought to teach henceforth France's dominant ideology, to use the Marxist expression unknown to Tocqueville himself? I am verging on the threshold of politics in the narrow sense of the term, a threshold I have hardly ever crossed and which I would not want to cross on this occasion. Allow me to quote a passage from a letter of Alexis de Tocqueville to John Stuart Mill which reveals another aspect of his thought and which would please the Justice Minister's companions:

> I do not need to tell you, my dear Mill, that the greatest malady which threatens a people organized as we are, is the gradual softening of mores, the lowering of the mind, the mediocrity of tastes. There lie the greatest

175

dangers of the future. A nation democratically constituted as ours is, where the natural vices of the people unfortunately coincide with those of civil society, cannot be allowed to adopt easily the habit of sacrificing the greatness it cherishes to its repose, or great things to petty things. It is not salutary for such a nation to let itself believe that its place in the world is smaller, that it has fallen from the rank where its fathers had placed it, and that it must seek its solace in building railways and in making prosper the well-being of each individual in a climate of peace, no matter how that peace be obtained. The leaders of such a nation must ever maintain a proud attitude if they do not wish to let the level of the nation's mores fall very low.[3]

This liberal struck a Gaullist tone every now and again. This prince of the mind did not turn his back on either the greatness of the country or the liberty of its citizens. He has been for a long time an isolated figure. Perhaps he is today bringing people together.

I could end on this note. But since the two speeches you have just heard deal with me as well as with this great man, I would like to say a few words about my own relations with him. His thought did not form mine. I read and I studied his books when I was teaching in the Sorbonne, at a point in life when the essentials of my philosophy of politics and human existence were fixed. *Democracy in America* helped me to understand the United States of our day and *The Ancien Régime and the Revolution* helped me to interpret the avatars of the French Republic. Tocqueville lived under five regimes. Everyone here present under forty years of age has known three. Yet, the road that led me to what is called my liberalism began with the critique of Marx and passed through the reading of Max Weber and the lived experience of totalitarian regimes. At the end of the road, I discovered Tocqueville and I was won over by the man as much as I was by the sociologist or the historian.

Why has there been such a rapport, such a friendship, between the Comte de Tocqueville and the university man, the intellectual, the grandson of a businessman in a Lorraine village, a Jew? I perceive at least one reason. I experience a kind of elective affinity for complex personalities, who are agreed on matters of principle but are troubled by doubt, who do not confuse the desirable with the probable or their tastes with reality, and who are aware of the constraints history imposes on us and the margin of freedom it leaves us. Tocqueville looked at America from the outside and was far from admiring it without reservation. He held it up as an example to the French, at least in certain respects. As an aristocrat by birth and by nature as well, he could not love democracy. Yet with his whole mind he subscribed to the democratic movement as irresistible and providential. He condemned himself to a thankless mediation between the reactionaries and the revolutionaries, even though that meant being rejected by both sides.

Perhaps I am even more moved by his correspondence with Gobineau. On July 20, 1856, he wrote to the author of the *Essay on the Inequality of the Races*: "I believe that your book's fortunes hang on its returning to France from abroad, especially through Germany. The Germans can provide you with a truly favorable audience. They are the only people in Europe who get excited over what they take to be true in the abstract without concerning themselves with its practical consequences. . . ." What a striking and tragic prophecy! Lastly, here are two passages from a letter of January 24, 1857: "With regard to the spirit of Christianity, its distinctive trait is to have sought to abolish all racial distinctions which the Jewish religion still allowed to subsist, and to fashion only one human species, all of whose members were equally capable of perfecting themselves and resembling one another. . . . Christianity manifestly has tended to make all men brothers and equals." A little further on Tocqueville writes: "In my eyes, human societies, like individuals, become something only by the use of liberty. . . . No, I will not believe that this human species which is at the head of visible creation has become that degenerate herd you tell us of and that there is nothing left but to surrender it, with no future and no recourse, to a small number of shepherds who are after all no better and often worse animals than we are. . . ."[4]

To his dying day, Alexis de Tocqueville refused to despair of the French, to disdain men, as his friend Arthur de Gobineau called on him to do. On the contrary, he took a profound and noble pleasure in following his principles, the liberty and the equality of men. Like so many others, I have been tempted in the past forty years by despair and disdain. I hope I have not succumbed. Every time I read Tocqueville's letters, I receive a lesson in courage, as though it came, across the years, from a teacher and a friend.

Translated by Marc LePain

Notes

1. This Appendix is Aron's acceptance speech on the occasion of his being awarded the first Tocqueville Prize in the fall of 1979 for works of Tocquevillean inspiration or character. The text originally appeared in *Commentaire* (3, Summer 1980). It appears here for the first time in English translation.

2. Aron is referring to the administration of Valéry Giscard D'Estaing, President of the French Fifth Republic from 1974 to 1981. (Editor's note)

3. This letter is dated March 18, 1841. The full letter can be found in Roger Boesche, ed. *Alexis de Tocqueville: Selected Letters on Politics and Society* (Berkeley: University of California Press, 1985), pp. 150–51. (Editor's note)

4. This letter is reproduced in full in Boesche, ed., *Alexis de Tocqueville: Selected Letters on Politics and Society,* pp. 342–48. (Editor's Note).

Selected Readings

Aron, Raymond. 1985. *Clausewitz: Philosopher of War.* Englewood Cliffs, N.J.: Prentice-Hall.

———. 1986. *Dimensions de la conscience historique.* Paris: Presses Pocket/Agora.

———. 1977. *Essai sur les libertés.* Paris: Pluriel.

———. 1989. *Essais sur la condition Juive contemporaine.* Paris: Editions de Fallois.

———. 1970. *An Essay on Freedom.* New York: World.

———. 1967. *Étapes de le pensée sociologique.* Paris: Gallimard.

———. 1972. *Études politiques.* Paris: Gallimard.

———. 1988. *Études sociologiques.* Paris: PUF.

———. 1985. *History, Truth, Liberty.* Ed. F. Draus. Chicago: University of Chicago Press.

———. 1938. *Introduction à la philosophie de l'histoire: Essai sur les limites de l'objectivé historique.* Paris: Gallimard.

———. 1961. *Introduction to the Philosophy of History: An Essay on the Limits of Historical Objectivity.* Boston: Beacon Press.

———. 1993. *Machiavel et les tyrannies modernes.* Ed. R. Freymond. Paris: Editions de Fallois.

———. 1968. *Main Currents in Sociological Thought. 1: Comte, Marx, Tocqueville, The Sociologists and the Revolution of 1848.* New York: Doubleday.

———. 1970. *Main Currents in Sociological Thought. 2: Durkheim, Pareto, Weber.* New York: Doubleday.

————. 1990. *Memoirs: Fifty Years of Political Reflection.* New York: Holmes & Meier.

————. 1957. *The Opium of the Intellectuals.* New York: Doubleday.

————. 1966. *Peace and War: A Theory of International Relations.* New York: Doubleday.

————. 1976. *Penser la Guerre: Clausewitz.* Vol. 1. L'âge europeén. Paris: Gallimard.

————. 1976. *Penser la Guerre: Clausewitz.* Vol. 2. L'âge planetaire. Paris: Gallimard.

————. 1978. *Politics and History.* Ed. M. Conant. New York: Free Press.

————. 1985. "Textes et temoignages." *Commentaire* 28 and 29.

Bavarez, Nicolas. 1993. *Raymond Aron: Un moraliste au temps des idéologies.* Paris: Flammarion.

Mahoney, Daniel J. 1992. *The Liberal Political Science of Raymond Aron: A Critical Introduction.* Lanham, Md.: Rowman & Littlefield.

Index

About the Editor

Daniel J. Mahoney is assistant professor of politics at Assumption College, Worcester, Massachusetts. He has written on Tocqueville and Aron and is presently completing a book entitled *DeGaulle: Statesmanship, Grandeur and Modern Democracy.* He is the author of *The Liberal Political Science of Raymond Aron* (Rowman & Littlefield, 1992).